Georg Möllerke · Engineering English

# Engineering English
Der Englischkurs
für Fachleute des Maschinenbaus

Mit Audio-CD

Zweite, erweiterte Auflage

Georg Möllerke

Zu diesem Buch gehört eine Audio-CD. Die im Inhaltsverzeichnis mit der CD-Positions-Nr. und im Text mit einem Stern (*) bezeichneten Artikel werden von professionellen Sprechern gelesen, danach folgt die Geschichte «The experiences of an engineer», bestehend aus fünf Episoden.

Sprecher für den Fachteil
Ian Cummings und (Mrs.) Jan Klingemann
Sprecher für «The experiences of an engineer»
Ronald Newman......... Ian Cummings
Anne Adams............ (Mrs.) Jan Klingemann
David Freeman.......... Paul Bendelow
Clark Kimball........... Michael Lucas
Brian Kent ............. Paul Bendelow
Patrick Hansen.......... Barry Jones
Paul Murray............. Michael Lucas

Idee und Ausarbeitung: Georg Möllerke,
El.-Ing. und staatl. gepr. Übersetzer
Als Lektor wirkte mit: Brian Rowntree, Masch.-Ing.

Folgende Bücher wurden ausgewertet:
Marine Steam Engines and Turbines
by S. C. McBirnie and W. J. Fox
Marine Diesel Engines
by C. C. Pounder
Marine Auxiliary Machinery
by E. Souchotte and D. W. Smith
Marine Electrical Practice
by G. O. Watson
All from Butterworth (Publishers) Ltd.
88 Kingsway, London WC2B 6AB
Mehrere Fachzeitschriften wurden
verwendet, vor allem:
New Scientist, London
Scientific American, New York
Engineering, London
Electronics & Power, Stevenage (GB)

Umschlagbild: mit freundlicher Genehmigung der Schloemann-Siemag AG, Düsseldorf

Die Deutsche Bibliothek – CIP-Einheitsaufnahme

Engineering English: der Englischkurs für Fachleute des
Maschinenbaus; mit Audio-CD/Georg Möllerke. –
Düsseldorf: VDI-Verl.
  ISBN 3-18-401543-2
NE: Moellerke, Georg

Buch. – 2., erw. Aufl. – 1996

CD. – 1996

© VDI-Verlag GmbH, Düsseldorf 1996

Alle Rechte, auch das des auszugsweisen Nachdruckes, der auszugsweisen oder vollständigen photomechanischen Wiedergabe (Photokopie, Mikrokopie), der elektronischen Datenspeicherung (Wiedergabesysteme jeder Art) und das der Übersetzung, vorbehalten.

Die Wiedergabe von Gebrauchsnamen, Handelsnamen, Warenbezeichnungen u. ä. in diesem Werk berechtigt auch ohne besondere Kennzeichnung nicht zu der Annahme, daß solche Namen im Sinne der Warenzeichen- und Markenschutz-Gesetzgebung als frei zu betrachten wären und daher von jedermann benutzt werden dürften.

Printed in Germany
Druck und Verarbeitung: Bonner Universitäts-Buchdruckerei
ISBN 3-18-401543-2

# Vorwort
## zur zweiten, erweiterten Auflage

Seit Erscheinen der Vorauflage hat das Interesse an diesem Kurs noch zugenommen, denn infolge der immer engeren internationalen Verflechtung von Technik und Wirtschaft verstärkt sich auch der Zwang für Ingenieure und Techniker, sich mit Geschäftspartnern im In- und Ausland auf Englisch zu verständigen. Dem trägt die vorliegende zweite Auflage Rechnung. Der Kurs wurde durch einen Lektüre-Teil mit fachbezogenen Texten wesentlich erweitert, wobei auf die Bildung eines praxisnahen Wortschatzes besonderer Wert gelegt wurde. Die zur Förderung einwandfreien Sprechens und des Hörverständnisses gedachte Audiokassette blieb inhaltlich unverändert, wurde aber durch eine Compact Disc (CD) ersetzt. Wir wünschen allen Benutzern, daß der Kurs ihnen weiterhin eine gute Hilfe bietet – sowohl bei der Alltagsarbeit wie auch zur Vorbereitung auf Dienstreisen, Fachtagungen, Seminare usw.

Nussbaumen/Schweiz und Düsseldorf,
im Juli 1996                                                    Verfasser und Verlag

# Vorwort

Dieser Englischkurs ist für Fachleute des Maschinenbaus und der Elektrotechnik bestimmt, die bereits über Grundkenntnisse der englischen Sprache verfügen.

Besonders wertvoll wird der Kurs durch die Sprecherrolle des englischen Schauspielers *Ian Cummings*. Er spricht in der Serie «The experiences of an engineer» die Rolle des Ingenieurs Ronald Newman. Sie hören mit der Kassette nicht nur einwandfreies Englisch, sondern auch angenehme Sprache. Engineering English ist ganz auf die Sprachbedürfnisse des Ingenieurs ausgerichtet. Fachgespräche, besonders im Umgang mit Kunden im Ausland sowie Korrespondenz, wie sie in Exportbetrieben typisch ist, haben Schwergewicht. Der Kurs unterstützt Fachleute bei ihrer täglichen Arbeit. Die einzelnen Abschnitte sind so bemessen, daß beim Lernen keine Langeweile aufkommen kann. Sehr hoffe ich, daß Engineering English auch Ihren Erwartungen entspricht.

Nussbaumen/Schweiz, im September 1990                    *Georg Möllerke*

# Vorwort

# Table of contents

|  | Page | CD-Pos. |
|---|---|---|

**Lesson 1**

1.1 Articles and demonstrative pronouns ........................................... 1
1.2 Organizing a meeting ........................................................... 3   1
1.3 Rating, power, output ........................................................... 4   2
1.4 Giant steam engine going strong after 77 years ................................ 5

**Lesson 2**

2.1 Interrogative pronouns ........................................................ 6
2.2 Alignment of a pump coupling ................................................. 7   3
2.3 Meeting the consulting engineer in your office .............................. 8   4
2.4 Taking the fog out of marine diesel engines .................................. 9

**Lesson 3**

3.1 Weak and strong verbs ......................................................... 10
3.2 How to avoid misunderstandings when handling specifications ............. 11   5
3.3 Technical letter ............................................................... 11
3.4 Letter openings and endings ................................................. 12

**Lesson 4**

4.1 Auxiliaries in short answers and agreements ................................ 14
4.2 Sliding feet of a turbine ..................................................... 15   6
4.3 Engineering terms used in describing metal plate working ................. 15
4.4 Mathematical formulae ........................................................ 17

**Lesson 5**

5.1 Sentence structure ............................................................ 18
5.2 Bedplate and frames of a marine diesel engine .............................. 18   7
5.3 Help required to perform a task ............................................. 19   8
5.4 Providing of equipment ....................................................... 20

**Lesson 6**

6.1 Present tenses ................................................................ 21
6.2 Checking the oil flow ......................................................... 21   9
6.3 Replacing bearing bushes ..................................................... 22   10
6.4 Erecting engineers replace bearing bushes .................................. 22
6.5 Technical periodical .......................................................... 23

|  | Page | CD-Pos |
|---|---|---|

**Lesson 7**

| 7.1 The past and perfect tenses | 24 | |
| 7.2 Cylinder liner of a marine diesel engine | 24 | 11 |
| 7.3 Starting a centrifugal pump | 25 | 12 |
| 7.4 On the telephone | 27 | 13 |
| 7.5 Watch the magnet for better ignition timing | 27 | |

**Lesson 8**

| 8.1 The future | 29 | |
| 8.2 Carbon glands for marine turbines | 30 | 14 |
| 8.3 Mounting equipment | 31 | |
| 8.4 Flow chart of a coal-fired power station | 33 | |
| 8.5 What a cracker | 34 | 15 |

**Lesson 9**

| 9.1 The participles | 35 | |
| 9.2 Lifting the turbine casing cover | 35 | 16 |
| 9.3 Melting is the secret of making joints | 36 | 17 |
| 9.4 Circuit diagram | 37 | 18 |
| 9.5 Selection procedure | 37 | |

**Lesson 10**

| 10.1 The gerund | 39 | |
| 10.2 Faulty control equipment | 40 | 19 |
| 10.3 Finnish company tackles a burning problem | 41 | 20 |
| 10.4 How to do a good job | 41 | |
| 10.5 Putting a tiger in your boiler | 42 | 21 |

**The experiences of an engineer**

| Episode 1 An erecting engineer relates his experiences abroad | 43 | 22 |
| Episode 2 Preliminary work on obtaining a major order | 44 | 23 |
| Episode 3 Meeting an important customer | 46 | 24 |
| Episode 4 Introducing a test engineer | 47 | 25 |
| Episode 5 Emergency call from Alaska | 48 | 26 |

**Focus on major engineering achievements**

| Cruise Vessel "Oriana" at 25 knots | 50 | |
| End of the line | 50 | |
| Staying ahead of the competition: Heidelberger Druckmaschinen AG | 51 | |
| Such is accuracy | 52 | |
| Keep an eye on the voltage level | 52 | |

Page

Fuel-cell engine ready for the industry .................................... 52
Significant reduction of diesel exhausts .................................... 53
MTU diesel engines for fast ferry .......................................... 54
Meteorite showered town with diamonds ...................................... 54
Increasing demand for cruise vessels ....................................... 55
Market for well-maintained engines ......................................... 55
American travellers abroad ................................................. 56
Low-speed engines for ship's propulsion .................................... 57
Saving millions on EU translations ......................................... 57
Panama Canal, an engineering marvel ........................................ 57
History lessons ............................................................ 58
Gas for UFO ................................................................ 58
Such is business ........................................................... 58
Being up to date ........................................................... 58
Mind your language ......................................................... 58
A stake in the company ..................................................... 60
Copping it from lead ....................................................... 60
America cracks down on illegal spy gear .................................... 61
DME fuel for future diesel engines ......................................... 61
World's largest factory building ........................................... 62
The Engineer's common language ............................................. 62
Electronic eyes unblinking ................................................. 63
Sweltering in the exhibition halls ......................................... 63
Race for pollution-free engines ............................................ 64
Put an end to toxic fuel ................................................... 64
When to transmit Mayday, when SOS? ......................................... 65
Strange place .............................................................. 65
Producing the licence ...................................................... 65
How strong is your car battery? ............................................ 66
Just for fun ............................................................... 66
Methane gas will fuel power stations ....................................... 67
How to handle specifications ............................................... 67
How to avoid misunderstandings when handling specifications ................ 67
Stopping the eavesdroppers ................................................. 69
Executive of an engineering company ........................................ 70
Two Concorde pilots ........................................................ 70
The fizzling of the "Queen Elizabeth 2" .................................... 71

**Phonetic alphabets** ..................................................... 72

# Lesson 1

# Unit 1.1

## Grammar from scratch
## Articles and demonstrative pronouns

### The definite article
The definite article is «the»:
the cylinder, the engine, the thrust bearing.

### The indefinite article
Before a word beginning with a consonant «a»:
a drilling machine, a cylinder, a thrust bearing.
Before a word beginning with a vowel «an»:
an engine, an engine-fitter, an actuator.

### Plurals
The plural is usually made by adding «s» to the singular:
The cylinders, the engines, the thrust bearings.

### Demonstrative adjectives and pronouns
The demonstrative adjectives and pronouns are:
this (singular)   these (plural)
that (singular)   those (plural)
Asking «What is this?» (cylinder liner), people of German mother tongue are inclined to answer «This is a cylinder liner» which is not right. In German one would say «Was ist dies (or: dieses, das)?» and answer «Dies (or: dieses, das) ist eine Zylinderlaufbuchse.»
I would like to emphasize, the answer in English must be «It is a cylinder liner». Showing this cylinder liner, without being asked, I would say «This is a cylinder liner».

What is this?

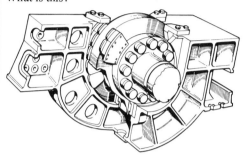

It is the thrust bearing of a marine diesel engine.

What is this?

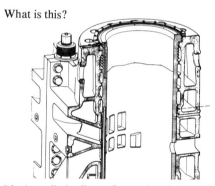

It's the cylinder liner of a marine diesel engine.

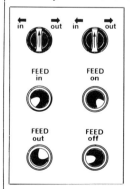

Those are control boxes.

1

What is this?

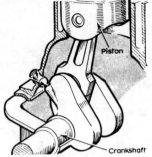

It's part of the driving mechanism of a four-stroke internal combustion engine.

Is this a boring machine?

Of course, it's not. It's a vertical drilling machine.

Is this man a designer?

Oh no, he doesn't look the designer type. He looks rather like an author.

Do you think the man with the cut-throat razor is a barber?

It's quite obvious, he's a barber. But he could also be an interrogator (US: pollster).

## Questions and answers

What is that?
It's a cylinder.
That's a cylinder.

What are these?
They are diesel engines.

What are those?
They're control boxes.

Is this a thrust bearing?
Yes, it is.
No, it's not a thrust bearing.

Are these boring machines?
Yes, they are.
No, they aren't.
No, they are drilling machines.

Is that a diesel engine?
No, that's not a diesel engine.
Yes, that's a diesel engine.

Are those cylinder liners?
Yes, they are.
No, they are not.
No, they aren't.
No, they are thrust bearings.

## Exercises
Change these sentences into the plural:
This is a marine diesel engine.

That's a thrust bearing.

What is this?

What is that?

*grammar* Grammatik - *from scratch* ganz von vorn, von Anfang an - *definite article* bestimmter Artikel - *cylinder* Zylinder - *engine* Motor, Maschine - *thrust bearing* Drucklager - *indefinite* unbestimmt - *consonant* Mitlaut, Konsonant - *drilling machine* Bohrmaschine - *vowel* Selbstlaut, Vokal - *engine-fitter* Maschinenschlosser - *actuator* Stellglied, Betätigungsorgan - *to add* anhängen, hinzufügen - *demonstrative adjectives and pronouns* Demonstrativ-Adjektive und -Pronomen - *mother tongue* Muttersprache - *inclined* geneigt - *to emphasize* betonen - *to show* zeigen *marine diesel engine* Schiffsdieselmotor - *part* Teil - *driving mechanism* Triebwerk - *four-stroke* Viertakt . . . - *internal combustion engine* Verbrennungskraftmaschine - *boring machine* Aufbohrmaschine - *drilling machine* Bohrmaschine (zum Bohren aus vollem Material) - *control box* Steuertafel - *designer* Konstrukteur - *rather* vielmehr, eher (als) - *cut-throat razor* Rasiermesser - *barber* Friseur - *obvious* offensichtlich, klar - *interrogator* Meinungsbefrager; US: pollster

# Unit 1.2

## Organizing a meeting*

*Let's arrange a meeting with the turbine section.*
Wir werden eine Besprechung mit der Turbinengruppe vorbereiten (oder: organisieren).
*Mr. Freeman wants to see us at ten fifteen.*
Mr. Freeman möchte uns um zehn Uhr fünfzehn sprechen.
*It won't take very long.*
Es wird nicht sehr lange dauern.
*I've tried to contact you all over the place.*
Ich habe überall versucht, Sie zu erreichen.
*I've arranged to see some customers this evening.*
Ich habe abgemacht, mich heute abend mit (einigen) Kunden zu treffen.
*Well, we mustn't keep you.*
In Ordnung, wir wollen Sie nicht (länger) aufhalten.
*This is just a very rough-and-ready guide to our new turbine control.*
Dieses ist nur eine grobe Vorstellung von unserer neuen Turbinensteuerung.
*I remember a talk with Mr. White a year ago about those GX controls.*
Ich erinnere mich an ein Gespräch vor einem Jahr mit Mr. White über diese GX-Steuerungen.
*We ought to draw up a short appraisal.*
Wir sollten eine kurzgefasste Abschätzung der Lage entwerfen.
*First of all we should tackle the control problem.*
Zuerst müssen wir mit dem Steuerungsproblem fertig werden.
*I felt all along that there was something wrong.*
Die ganze Zeit dachte ich schon, dass da etwas nicht richtig sein könnte.
*We mustn't get confused by these findings.*
Wir sollten uns wegen dieser Feststellung nicht verwirren lassen.

3

## Exercises

Form full sentences:
1. Diesel engine 2500 bhp, 1800 rev/min.
2. Turbine 600 MW, 3000 rev/min.
3. Electric motor 240 kW, 820 rev/min.

*rating* Leistung; sonst auch: Bemessung, Bewertung, Abschätzung - *power* Leistung (bei Maschinen), Antriebskraft, Stärke, Leistungsfähigkeit - *output* (abgegebene) Leistung; sonst auch: Produktion, Ausstoss, Ertrag - *turbocharged* turbogeladen, mit Turbogebläse aufgeladen - *compact* gedrungen, kompakt - *design* Ausführung, Konstruktion - *two-stroke* Zweitakt... - *four-stroke* Viertakt... - *available* erhältlich, verfügbar, auf dem Markt - *v form* V-Form (V-Motor) - *in-line form* «Reihenausführung» (Reihenmotor) - *engine* Motor; sonst auch: Maschine - *bore* Bohrung - *stroke* (Kolben-)Hub - *to cover* umfassen, abdecken - *range* Bereich - *bhp* brake horse-power: Nutzleistung in PS, Bremsleistung in PS - *drawing* Zeichnung - *cross-section* Querschnitt (Schnittzeichnung) - *performance* (see below) Verrichtung, Ausführung, Erfüllung (Pflicht, Versprechen), Aufführung (Theater)

## Please note

Do not use «performance» in this connection although this term can be found for «Leistung» in some dictionaries. «Performance» as per Webster's Dictionary of the American Language: 1. accomplishment, execution, act of performing 2. operating or functioning, usually with regard to effectiveness, as of a machine 3. something done or performed, deed or feat.

# Unit 1.3

## Rating, power, output*

The Sulzer Z engines are turbo-charged and of compact design. Both two-stroke and four-stroke versions are available in V form as well as in in-line form. The engines have a bore of 400 mm and a stroke of 480 mm and cover an output range of 2500 bhp to 9600 bhp. This drawing shows the cross-section of the V-type design.

## Alternatively used expressions

The Z engine is rated at 9600 bhp, 1800 rev/min.
The engine has a rating (or: output) of...
The engine develops (or: produces, generates)...
The rated output of the engine is...

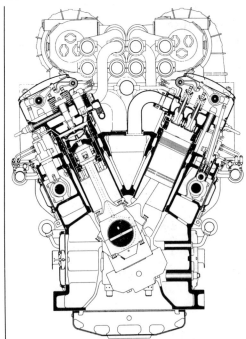

Cross section of a Sulzer ZBV marine diesel engine.

# Unit 1.4

## Giant steam engine going strong after 77 years

Probably the oldest steam engine used for driving a mine hoist is still earning its keep at the Jagersfontain diamond mine in the Union of South Africa. It is a Yates and Thom, double-expansion, vertical engine of 2500 hp, directly connected to a 12 ft. diameter cable drum. Since installation in 1902, it has handled around 50 million tons of material in its two skips. And only once has a major breakdown occured; in 1954 when its crankshaft fractured. In 1916 the engine held a world record for hauling 1000 tons of material an hour for 8 hours. At that time, it was permitted to run at 3500 ft. per minute, while hauling a 10-ton load from 900 ft. below the surface.
As Jagersfontain mine is nearing the end of its working life, no attempt will be made to replace this steam-driven winding equipment, but that may not be for another five years.
(Power, New York)

*giant steam engine* Riesendampfmaschine - *going strong* immer noch in vollem Einsatz - *probable (-bly)* wahrscheinlich - *to drive* (an)treiben - *mine hoist* Förderanlage - *is still earning its keep* macht sich immer noch bezahlt - *diamond mine* Diamantenmine, -grube - *double-expansion vertical engine* vertikale Doppelexpansions-Dampfmaschine - *hp* horse-power - *directly connected* direkt gekuppelt - *diameter* Durchmesser - *cable drum* Seiltrommel, Kabeltrommel - *to handle* umschlagen, fördern; sonst auch: handhaben - *skip* (Förder-)Kübel - *major breakdown* grössere Betriebsstörung - *to occur* auftreten - *crankshaft* Kurbelwelle - *to fracture* brechen, zu Bruch gehen - *to haul* fördern - *to permit* gestatten - *load* Ladung, Last - *surface* (Erd-)Oberfläche - *attempt* Versuch - *to replace* ersetzen - *steam-driven* dampfgetrieben - *winding equipment* Förderanlage

**My Sahara-Crossing Slimming holidays are a huge success. Package tours without food, drink or accommodation are available from Fr. 3000 per week.**

# Lesson 2

## Unit 2.1

### Interrogative pronouns

Interrogative pronouns (Fragefürwörter) for persons
Nominative: who
Accusative: whom, who
Possessive: whose (pronoun and adjective)

Interrogative pronouns for things
Nominative: what (pronoun and adjective)
Accusative: what (pronoun and adjective)

Interrogative pronouns for things or persons when the choice is restricted
Nominative: which (pronoun and adjective)
Accusative: which (pronoun and adjective)

### Sample sentences

Who took my spanner? Henry took it.
Who are those men? They are mechanical engineers from GEC.
Who (or: whom) did you see? I saw the designer.
Who did they speak to? (or: to whom did they speak?)
They spoke to the chief engineer.
Whose hammers are these? They are Brian's.
Whose are these? They are Alan's.
Whose car is this? It is mine.
What papers do you read? I read «The Mechanical Engineer».
Which university did he go to, Oxford or Cambridge?
He went to Oxford.

Who is this lady?

This lady is a detective.

Who are they?

They are researchers, except for the subject on the left.

## Exercises

Form other legends to these pictures.

*choice* Wahl - *restricted* eingeschränkt, beschränkt - *sample sentence* Mustersatz - *spanner* (Mutter-)Schlüssel, Bolzenschlüssel - *mechanical engineer* Maschinenbau-Ingenieur - *designer* Konstrukteur - *chief engineer* Leitender Ingenieur, Chefingenieur, (Technischer) Abteilungsleiter - *researcher* Forscher - *except (for)* ausgenommen

# Unit 2.2

## Alignment of a pump coupling *

The coupling should be aligned after the erection work is finished. Misalignment is to be corrected by placing shims underneath the pump driver as required. Simultaneously the specified clearance between the coupling halves must be maintained around the complete circumference. Measurements should be made at diametral positions – top bottom, sides – using a slip gauge. For flexible couplings alignment may be considered as being acceptable if a straight-edge, when placed parallel to the shaft across the coupling halves, rests along the whole width of both surfaces. This must be confirmed by repeated checks at several points around the whole circumference.

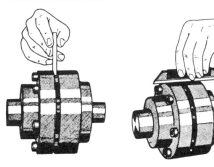

*alignment* Ausrichten; sonst auch: Anordnung, Anpassung - *coupling* Kupplung - *to align* ausrichten, ausfluchten - *erection work* Montage, Aufstellungsarbeit - *to finish* beenden, fertigstellen, zu Ende führen - *misalignment* Ausrichtfehler, schlechtes Ausrichten - *to correct* korrigieren - *to place* legen, plazieren - *shim* Blechscheibe, Blechzwischenlage - *underneath* unter, darunter - *driver* hier: Antriebsmotor - *required* erforderlich, notwendig - *simultaneous(ly)* gleichzeitig - *specified* spezifiziert, nach Aufstellungsvorschrift - *clearance* Abstand, Spiel(raum) - *halves* Hälften; Sing.: half - *to maintain* (bei)behalten, (aufrecht)erhalten - *circumference* Umfang, Peripherie - *measurement* Messung - *diametral* (genau) entgegengesetzt - *top* oben - *bottom* unten - *slip gauge* (US: gage) Fühlerlehre - *to consider* betrachten, erwägen - *acceptable* annehmbar - *straight-edge* Haarlineal - *shaft* Welle - *to rest* legen, auflegen - *width* Breite - *surface* Fläche, Oberfläche - *to confirm* hier: nachprüfen, überprüfen; sonst: bestätigen - *repeated* wiederholt

### Verbs used in the description

*align* ausrichten, ausfluchten
*confirm* vergewissern, bestätigen; hier auch: verify
*consider* betrachten, erwägen; hier auch: regard, judge
*correct* korrigieren; hier auch: rectify, adjust, eliminate
*finish* beenden; hier auch: complete, carry out
*maintain* (bei)behalten, (aufrecht)erhalten; hier auch: set, uphold
*place* legen, plazieren; hier auch: lay, locate, position
*rest* auflegen; hier auch: place, lay
*use* verwenden; hier auch: employ

### Alternatively used terms

*erection work* assembly work - *slip gauge* feeler gauge - *coupling half* hub

### Exercises

This lecture offers one way of expressing imperative structures using «to be», another is to

7

form direct imperative sentences as applied in instruction manuals and operator handbooks. For example: Align the coupling after the erection work is finished. Correct any misalignment by placing shims under the pump driver as required...
Convert further sentences from the description to the direct imperative.

# Unit 2.3

## Meeting the consulting engineer in your office*

*Good afternoon Mr. Russell, I'm Mrs. Zumbrunn.*
Guten Tag Mr. Russell, Ich bin Frau Zumbrunn.

*You've been here before, I assume.*
Sie waren schon einmal hier, nehme ich an.

*Yes, three times. Last time I came here I met Mr. Ineichen.*
Ja, dreimal. Als ich das letzte Mal hier war, sprach ich mit Herrn Ineichen.

*Would you like a cup of coffee or something to eat?*
Hätten Sie gern eine Tasse Kaffee oder etwas zu essen?

*I could do with a cup of coffee.*
Eine Tasse Kaffee könnte ich gebrauchen.

*How long do you intend staying with us?*
Wie lange beabsichtigen Sie bei uns zu bleiben?

*I'll be here for seven days this time. I must be back in Edinburgh by Wednesday at the latest.*
Ich bleibe diesmal für sieben Tage hier. Ich muss spätestens bis Mittwoch in Edinburgh zurück sein.

*I hope, you'll bring Mr. Edwards with you next time.*
Das nächste Mal, hoffe ich, bringen Sie Mr. Edwards mit.

*How has production progressed since my last visit?*
Wie ist es mit der Fertigung vorangegangen seit meinem letzten Besuch?

*All machining has been completed, and the unit is now being assembled.*
Mit der Bearbeitung sind wir fertig, die Maschine wird jetzt zusammengebaut.

*Will you be able to meet the planned delivery dates?*
Werden Sie die geplanten Ablieferungstermine einhalten können?

*Assuming the tests are successfully completed, yes.*
Angenommen, die Prüfungen werden erfolgreich abgeschlossen, ja.

*Before I go, could you show me those test results again?*
Könnten Sie mir nochmals die Prüfungsergebnisse zeigen bevor ich gehe?

*Actually, I can let you have a copy if you wish.*
Ich könnte Ihnen (eigentlich) auch eine Kopie anfertigen lassen, falls Sie eine wünschen.

*Would you like to visit the test bay today?*
Möchten Sie das Prüffeld heute (noch) sehen?

*I don't think I'll be able to fit it in today, but perhaps during my next visit.*
Ich glaube nicht, dass die Zeit hierfür heute noch reicht, aber vielleicht während meines nächsten Besuches.

**Engineering Report readers won't stand aside.**

# Unit 2.4

## Taking the fog out of marine diesel engines

Two or three times every year a marine diesel explodes as a result of a build-up of a fine oil mist in the engine's crank case. Most modern large marine diesels have precautions such as tighter seals to reduce oil leaks, special vents and continuous monitoring devices – which detect when the oil/air mixture reaches an explosive level and sound an alarm – but it is difficult to stop oil mist occurring.

Now Harris Engineering Ltd of Tunbridge Wells has developed a device it calls a vent fog precipitator, which uses electrostatic precipitation to remove oil particles down to 0.1 micron. Air from the crank case first passes through a mechanical filter which takes out any large particles or grit, then to an ionising section consisting of a metal tube with a fine tungsten wire running centrally inside it. The wire has a constant dc current at a potential of 10 000 volts and the potential difference between it and the tube causes the gas to ionise.

The air flow takes the oil particles, now positively charged, upwards to a collecting unit. Here the tube wall has a strong negative charge to which the ionised particles are attracted. Oil accumulates on the tube walls and runs down through a trap, back to the gear case. According to Harris, the unit operates with 90 per cent efficiency and can be applied to a range of other industrial situations.
(The Motorship, London)

*to take out* herausbringen, herausnehmen - *fog* Nebel - *marine diesel engine* Schiffsdieselmotor - *times* mal - *to explode* explodieren - *result* Ergebnis, Resultat - *build up* Aufbau, Entwicklung - *oil mist* Öldunst - *crank case* Kurbelgehäuse - *precaution* Vorkehrung, Vorsichtsmassnahme - *tight* festsitzend, dicht - *seal* Dichtung - *to reduce* verringern, reduzieren - *oil leak* Ölleck - *vent* Entlüftung, Entlüftungsöffnung - *continuous* Dauer..., dauernd, laufend - *monitoring device* Überwachungsgerät - *to detect* feststellen, aufspüren - *mixture* Mischung - *explosive level* explosionsgefährdeter Punkt - *to sound* ertönen (lassen) - *difficult* schwierig - *to occur* auftreten
*to develop* entwickeln - *to call* nennen - *vent fog precipitator* Dunstabscheider; precipitator auch: Ausfällapparat - *tu use* verwenden - *precipitation* Abscheidung, Fällung - *to remove* entfernen - *to pass through* durchströmen - *grit* hier: feste Bestandteile; sonst: grober Sand, Kies - *ionising section* Ionisierungsteil - *to consist of* bestehen aus - *metal tube* Metallrohr - *tungsten wire* Wolframdraht - *central(ly)* in der Mitte - *dc* (or: d.c.) direct current: Gleichstrom - *to cause* bewirken - *to ionise* ionisieren
*air flow* Luftstrom - *positively charged* positiv geladen - *upwards* hinauf - *collecting unit* Sammelgerät - *tube wall* Rohrwandung - *charge* Ladung, Auflagung - *to attract* anziehen - *to accumulate* (sich) sammeln - *trap* hier: Auffangtopf; sonst: Falle - *gear case* hier: Kurbelgehäuse; sonst: Getriebekasten - *according to* gemäss - *to operate* arbeiten - *efficiency* Wirkungsgrad - *to apply* anwenden, verwenden - *range* Reihe, Bereich

**You'll forget the world around you – when reading Engineering Report**

# Lesson 3

## Unit 3.1

### Weak and strong verbs

**Verbs, weak and regular**
operate, operated, operated
enter, entered, entered
The verbs are marked by ending -ed in the past (Präteritum = Vergangenheit) as well as in the past participle tense (Partizip Perfekt = Mittelwort der Vergangenheit).

**Verbs, weak and irregular**
send, sent, sent
These kind of weak verbs are all those not ending with -ed, except some in the past tense, and which do not change their vowel.

**Verbs, strong and irregular**
give, gave, given
begin, began, begun
These verbs change their original vowel.

**The weak and irregular verbs can be split into three groups**
a) All forms identical
bid, bid, bid
burst, burst, burst
cost, cost, cost
shut, shut, shut
b) Past and participle identical
bend, bent, bent
build, built, built
learn, learnt, learnt
send, sent, sent
c) Past with -ed
show, showed, shown
saw, sawed, sawn
mow, mowed, mown

I operate the electronic stove
you operate the electronic stove
he operates the electronic stove
she operates the electronic stove
we operate the electronic stove
you operate the electronic stove
they operate the electronic stove

### Exercises
Complete the conjugations.
I operate the coffee machine.
you operate ...
I enter the office
you enter ...

*weak* schwach - *regular* regelmässig - *to operate* arbeiten (an, bei), betreiben - *to enter* eintreten (in), betreten - *to mark* kennzeichnen; sonst auch: markieren - *irregular* unregelmässig - *to send* senden, schicken - *except* ausgenommen - *to change* ändern - *vowel* Vokal, Selbstlaut - *original* ursprünglich - *to split* aufteilen; sonst auch: spalten - *identical* identisch, gleich - *to bid* (an)bieten, Preisangebot machen - *to burst* platzen - *to bend* biegen - *to build* bauen - *to learn* lernen, erfahren - *to show* zeigen, *to saw* sägen - *to mow* mähen - *stove* Herd, Ofen

# Unit 3.2

## How to avoid misunderstandings when handling specifications*

Even with accurately written specifications, misunderstandings can occur. One means of preventing misreadings is to include key drawings which provide a basis for discussion on specific points. Building and layout plans can be regarded as key plans, as can also one-line diagrams for electrical systems. It is easier to talk to your counterpart on the telephone about the equipment if both of you have the same plans with comprehensive information in front of you, not just a written text. Sometimes people call up who have difficulty expressing themselves clearly in English. Plans which contain plenty of detail will help to overcome possible communication problems. A customer will be impressed if he receives the information he wants without delay. Furthermore, a detailed question can be answered without having too much paper on the table. It is of great advantage to use scaled-down plans. However, great care must be taken that lettering of suitable size is used. The information on the reduced diagram or sketch might otherwise be illegible.

*to avoid* vermeiden - *misunderstandings* Missverständnisse - *to handle* umgehen mit, behandeln, handhaben - *specification* Bauvorschrift, Pflichtenheft, Spezifikation - *even* sogar, selbst - *accurate(ly)* sorgfältig, genau - *to prevent* vermeiden, verhindern - *misreadings* falsches (Ab-) Lesen - *to include* einbeziehen, einschliessen - *key drawing* Schlüsselplan - *to provide* vorsehen, liefern - *building and layout plans* Gebäude- und Anordnungspläne - *to regard* betrachten - *one-line diagram* Übersichtsplan (elektrisch) - *counterpart* Gegenüber; sonst auch: Gegenstück - *equipment* Ausrüstung, Anlage, Gerät(e) - *comprehensive* umfassend, inhaltsreich - *to express* (sich) ausdrücken - *to contain* enthalten, umfassen - *detail* Einzelheit - *to overcome* fertigwerden (mit) - *communication problems* Verständigungsschwierigkeiten - *customer* Kunde - *impressed* beeindruckt - *to receive* erhalten - *delay* Verzögerung - *detailed* detailliert - *advantage* Vorteil - *scaled-down* in verkleinertem Massstab - *lettering* Buchstaben(auswahl) - *suitable* passend, geeignet - *size* Grösse - *reduced* verkleinert; sonst auch: reduziert - *diagram* (Schalt-)Plan, Diagramm - *illegible* unleserlich

# Unit 3.3

## Technical letter
### Re: Flowmeters for low gas flows

Dear Sirs,
We have learned from your advertisement published in «Mechanics & Power» that your company also offers flowmeters suitable for low gas flows.
As a manufacturer of monitoring equipment for the chemical industry, we are naturally very interested in all types of flowmeters, especially in those measuring small volumes and low flow rates of gases. Please forward us a copy of your new catalogue as soon as possible.
Thanking you in anticipation
    Yours faithfully,
    Biggs Monitoring Ltd.

*flowmeter* Strömungsmesser, Durchflussmesser - *low gas flows* geringe Gasströmungen (oder: Gasmengen) - *to learn* hier: erfahren - *advertisement* Inserat - *to publish* veröffentlichen - *to offer* (an)bieten - *suitable* geeignet - *manufacturer* Hersteller - *monitoring equipment* Überwachungsgerät(e); equipment auch: Ausrüstung, Anlage(n) - *chemical industry* Chemieindustrie - *natural(ly)* natürlich, selbstverständlich - *especial(ly)* besonders, speziell - *to measure* messen - *to forward* (über)senden - *thanking you in anticipation* mit bestem Dank im voraus; anticipation auch: Erwartung

# Unit 3.4

## Letter openings and endings

### Letter openings

*Thank you very much for your immediate reply to our questions.*
Wir danken Ihnen sehr für die sofortige Beantwortung unserer Fragen.

*We are very pleased to note from your letter of 2nd May...*
Wir freuen uns, aus Ihrem Brief vom 2. Mai zu erfahren...

*Thank you very much for your letter of 20th May regarding...*
Vielen Dank für Ihren Brief vom 20. Mai betreffend...

*In reply to your letter of 3rd April, we have pleasure in offering you...*
Wir freuen uns, Ihnen gemäss Brief vom 3. April... anbieten zu können.

*We regret to learn from your report...*
Wir bedauern, Ihrem Bericht entnehmen zu müssen...

*In response to your request of 19th May, I would advise you...*
Entsprechend Ihrer Anfrage (oder: Ihres Gesuches) möchte ich Ihnen mitteilen (oder: raten, empfehlen)...

*I am delighted to tell you...*
Es freut mich, Ihnen mitteilen zu können...

*This is to let know...*
Hiermit möchten wir Sie informieren...

*I am sorry to have to tell you...*
Es tut mir leid, Ihnen mitteilen zu müssen...

*I must write you a few words of thanks for...*
Ich muss Ihnen ein paar Worte des Dankes wegen (oder: für)... schreiben.

*Thanking you for your above mentioned enquiry, we take pleasure in quoting you for...*
Wir danken Ihnen für die oben erwähnte Anfrage und möchten Ihnen folgendes Angebot unterbreiten:...

*In accordance with your request, we submit the following quotation:...*
Gemäss Ihrer Anfrage übersenden wir folgende Offerte:...

*We have much pleasure in attaching...*
Es freut uns, Ihnen als Beilage... übersenden zu können.

*Please provide additional data providing the background information and parameters which went into this calculation.*
Übersenden Sie bitte weitere grundsätzliche Angaben und Parameter, die dieser Berechnung zugrunde gelegt worden sind.

*This letter confirms our verbal acceptance given to you on the 5th May at your offices.*
Mit diesem Brief bestätigen wir unsere mündliche Zusage vom 5. Mai in Ihrem Hause.

*Following a discussion with your Mr. Jones on ... at ...*
Gemäss einer Diskussion mit Ihrem Herrn Jones am... in...

*Would you be so kind as to allow me to bring this matter to your notice.*
Gestatten Sie bitte, dass ich mich in dieser Angelegenheit an Sie wende.

*It is understood that you have been favoured with an order for (the delivery of) eight 600 MW turbo-generator sets.*
Uns wurde bekannt, dass Sie einen Auftrag für acht 600 MW-Turbogeneratorsätze erhalten haben.

### Letter endings

*We trust that we have been of some assistance in this matter.*
Wir hoffen, dass wir Ihnen in dieser Angelegenheit einige Unterstützung geben konnten.

*If you require any further information, please do not hesitate to contact us.*
Falls Sie weitere Angaben (oder: Unterlagen) benötigen, so setzen Sie sich bitte mit uns in Verbindung.

*We shall be glad to supply any further information which may be required.*
Gern übersenden wir Ihnen weitere Unterlagen, falls erforderlich.

*Thanking you in anticipation for . . .*
Vielen Dank im voraus für . . .

*We should be glad if you would accept our proposal and hope to hear from you soon.*
Wir würden uns freuen, wenn Sie unseren Vorschlag annehmen würden und hoffen bald wieder (etwas) zu hören.

*We should be very obliged if you could furnish us the . . .*
Wir wären Ihnen sehr dankbar, wenn Sie uns die . . . übersenden könnten.

*We trust that our explanation will convince you . . .*
Wir hoffen, dass unsere Erklärung Sie (davon) überzeugt . . .

*When you have received the information, we naturally would be interested in getting the benefit of your opinion.*
Wenn Sie die Unterlagen erhalten haben, so hätten wir gern Ihre Meinung hierüber erfahren.

*We would appreciate receiving a copy of your new catalogue at your earliest convenience.*
Wir würden uns sehr freuen, wenn Sie uns umgehend Ihren neuen Katalog zustellen könnten.

*We look forward to hearing from you again.*
Wir würden uns sehr freuen, von Ihnen wieder etwas zu hören.

**Motorists remember: It requires skill to drive a car with caravan.**

# Lesson 4

# Unit 4.1

## Auxiliaries in short answers and agreements

Auxiliaries (Hilfszeitwörter) are extremely important in conversation because in short answers, agreements, disagreements with remarks and additions to remarks we use auxiliaries instead of repeating the original verb.

### Auxiliaries in short answers

Questions requiring the answer «yes» or «no», i.e. such as, «Do you smoke?» or «Can you ride a bicycle?», should be answered by «yes» or «no» and the auxiliary only. The original subject, if a noun, is replaced by a pronoun.
Do you smoke? Yes, I do (not: Yes, I smoke).
Can the engineer cook? No, he can't.
Has Tom an oscilloscope? Yes, he has.
May I go? Yes, you may.
Must he go? Yes, he must (or: No, he needn't).

### Agreements and disagreements with remarks

Agreements with affirmative (bejahend) remarks are made similarly, with «yes», «so», or «of course». If there is an auxiliary in the first verbs this auxiliary is repeated; if there is no auxiliary, «do/does» is used in the present and «did» in the past.
It is very cold in here. Yes, it is.
This protective helmet is too small for you. Yes, it is.
He may give us some tools. Yes, he may.
Mr. Biggs and Mr. White go to New York every year. Yes, they do.
The erecting engineers left home yesterday. Yes, they did.
Agreements with negative remarks are made with «no» and negative auxiliaries.
The designers didn't like it. No, they didn't.
The manager isn't old. No, he isn't.
We haven't much time. No, we haven't.
The engineer will hurt himself. No, he won't.
Why did you go to London yesterday? But I didn't.
The electrician lent you the tool. No, he didn't.

### Other examples

He won't come. Oh, yes, he will.
You can't do it. Yes, I can.
The boat didn't capsize. Oh, yes, it did.

### Exercises

Form questions and answer «yes» or «no» using auxiliaries, e.g.:
Has Henry a screwdriver? Yes, he has.
Roger has an oscilloscope ...
The electrician must go now ...
The manager can cook ...
Henry has enough time for repairing his watch?

This egg is rather big, isn't it?
This egg is rather big. Yes, it is.
This egg beats all records, doesn't it?
This egg isn't ours, is it?

# Unit 4.2

## Sliding feet of a turbine*

The feet of the forward end of the casing are designed in such a way as to permit free axial expansion but no vertical movement. Provision must be made for lubrication.
Turbine casings have been known to fracture when the lubrication of the sliding faces of the feet was neglected. They become firmly rusted together preventing end movement and thereby putting a high stress on the casing. A position indicator should be fitted to indicate the relative movement between the casing and the seating. The position of the pointer is used as a guide to the thermal state of the turbine during the warming up period prior to starting.

*sliding feet* Gleitfüsse, Gleitstücke - *forward end* Vorderseite - *casing* Gehäuse - *to design* anordnen, vorsehen, konstruieren - *to permit* gestatten - *expansion* Ausdehnung - *movement* Bewegung - *provision* Möglichkeit, Vorkehrung - *lubrication* Schmierung - *case* Fall - *to fracture* zu Bruch gehen, brechen - *sliding face* Gleitfläche - *to neglect* vernachlässigen - *firm (ly)* fest - *to rust together* zusammenrosten - *to prevent* verhindern - *stress* (mechanische) Spannung - *position indicator* Anzeigegerät - *to fit* anbringen, anbauen - *to indicate* anzeigen - *seating* Sitzfläche, Lagerung - *guide* hier: Richtlinie - *thermal state* Erwärmungszustand - *warming up period* Vorwärmzeit - *prior to* vor

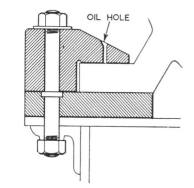

Fastened sliding foot

### Verbs used in the description

*design* anordnen, gestalten, konstruieren
*fit* anbringen, anbauen
*fracture* zu Bruch gehen, brechen;
    hier auch: damage, crack
*indicate* anzeigen, bezeichnen; hier auch: measure, show
*neglect* vernachlässigen, unterlassen, missachten; hier auch: disregard, ignore
*permit* gestatten
*prevent* verhindern
*use* verwenden; hier auch: act

### Alternatively used terms

*provision must be made* means must be provided - *to put a high stress* to exercise a high stress - *movement* play - *state* condition - *tell-tale pointer* movement indicator, slide indicator, position indicator

# Unit 4.3

## Engineering terms used in describing metal plate working

The control console (right) is provided with:
*round holes* runde Löcher; oder: Rundlöcher, runde Ausschnitte
*square holes* quadratische Löcher
*rectangular holes* rechteckige Löcher
*drill holes* Bohrlöcher

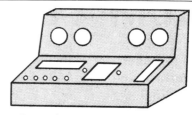

Control console.

*The instruments must fit with minimum clearance into the square holes of the panel.*
Die Instrumente müssen mit einem minimalen Spielraum in die quadratischen Löcher der Tafel passen.

*Remove all devices and dowel pins before painting the door glossy white.*
Alle Geräte und Passstifte sind zu entfernen, bevor die Tür weissglänzend gestrichen wird.

*Before starting production, all sheet metal to be used is to be plate-gauge checked.*
Bevor die Produktion aufgenommen wird, sind alle Bleche, die verwendet werden sollen, mit einer Blechlehre zu prüfen.

*10.2 mm diameter holes are to be provided (or: arranged) in the corners of the plate.*
Löcher mit einem Durchmesser von 10,2 mm sind in den Ecken der Platte vorzusehen (oder: anzuordnen).

*The holes for the toggle switches are not to be greater than 20.1 mm in diameter (see tolerance chart).*
Die Löcher für die Kippschalter dürfen nicht grösser als 20,1 mm im Durchmesser sein (siehe Toleranztabelle).

*The rectangular cut-outs are to be checked for accuracy with a jig.*
Die rechteckigen Ausschnitte sind mit einer Schablone auf Genauigkeit zu prüfen.

*Deburr all sides carefully using the new Burdy & White device in order to achieve uniform chamfering.*
Alle Seiten sind sorgfältig mit dem neuen Burdy & White-Gerät zu entgraten, um gleichmässige Schrägkanten zu erhalten.

*Cut-outs for the flush-mounted XY units must be milled out in order to obtain the close (or: fine, tight) tolerances required.*
Ausschnitte für die bündig abschneidenden XY-Geräte müssen ausgefräst werden, um die erforderlichen engen Toleranzen zu erhalten.

**Please note**
Bei Blechbearbeitungen wird empfohlen, «deburr» (für entgraten) zu verwenden, da «flash» (oft in Wörterbüchern angegeben), sich auf schwere Stücke bezieht, zum Beispiel auf Gussstücke. Für «Löcher» oder «Bohrungen» nicht «aperture» einsetzen, da dieses Wort hauptsächlich die Bedeutung von «Öffnung» und «Blende» hat. Für «Ausschnitt» nicht «recess» verwenden; die Bedeutung ist vorwiegend «Vertiefung» und «Absatz».

---

Kurt Simon
**Englisch für Ingenieure in Studium und Praxis**
2., neubearb. Aufl. 1996.
150 S. DIN A5. Br.
DM 38,00/öS 296,00/sFr 38,00
ISBN 3-18-401571-8

Dem Leser wird in lockerer Form Hilfestellung gegeben, um einstmals Gelerntes aufzufrischen, zu vertiefen und ihn zum Gebrauch der englischen Sprache hinzuführen. Der erste Teil des Buches wiederholt Grammatik und Aussprache, der zweite Teil bietet Tips zur Erarbeitung eines persönlichen Wortschatzes. Im dritten Teil werden Texte aus dem technischen und wissenschaftlichen Bereich ausführlich durchgearbeitet und kommentiert. Teil vier gibt Anleitungen zum Ausarbeiten eines Textes, Vortrags oder Referats in englischer Sprache.

Postfach 10 10 54, 40001 Düsseldorf
Telefon 02 11/61 88-0, Telefax 02 11/61 88-133

# Unit 4.4
## Mathematical formulae

$x^{-1} \cdot x^3$
x to the power (of) minus one times x cubed

$x^0 \cdot x^2$
x to the power (of) zero times x squared

$x^{-2} \cdot x^4$
x to the power (of) minus two times x to the power (of) four

$x^1 \cdot \sqrt[2]{x}$
x to the power (of) one times square root (of) x

$\sqrt[3]{x} \cdot \sqrt[4]{x}$
cube root (of) x times fourth root (of) x

$P = I^2 \cdot R$
P equals I squared times R

$I = \dfrac{U}{R_g}$
I equals U over R sub (small) g

$\dfrac{R_N}{R_M} = \dfrac{I_M}{I_N}$
R sub (capital) N over R sub (capital) M equals I sub (capital) M over I sub (capital) N

$A = \dfrac{M \cdot v^2}{2}$
A equals M times v squared, all over 2

$U = \sqrt{3} \cdot U_p$
U equals (square) root (of) 3 times U sub (small) p

$h = \dfrac{v \cdot t}{2} = \dfrac{g \cdot t^2}{2}$
h equals v times t, all over two, equals g times t squared, all over two

$R_t = \dfrac{u_t \, U^2 \, 10^4}{S_n}$
(capital) R sub (small) t equals (small) u sub t times (capital) U squared times 10 to the fourth, all over (capital) S sub (small) n (or: ... fourth power; power of four)

$\int ax \, dx = a \int x \, dx$
$= \dfrac{a\,x^2}{2} + C$
integral of ax dx equals a times integral of x dx equals a times x squared all over two, plus C

$\left(\dfrac{a}{b} c + d\right)$
a over b times c, plus d, all in parentheses

$\displaystyle\int_{x_a}^{x_b} \dfrac{I_p{}^3}{p + I_n{}^{-3}} \, dx$
integral between the limits x sub a and x sub b of I sub p cubed, over p plus I sub n to the (power of) minus three, times dx

Bei Potenzen auch: $x^n$ = x to the power n, x to the nth power, x raised to n

"I'll tell you what – keep your free rust and knock twenty pounds off."
(Punch, London)

# Lesson 5

## Unit 5.1

### Sentence structure and word order

The word order in the English language is more rigidly given than in the German. The normal order in a sentence is in the affirmative (Aussagesatz) and interrogative sentence (Fragesatz), in the principal clause (Hauptsatz) and subordinate clause (Nebensatz):

### Subject - Verb - Object

*The engineer presses the key.*
Der Ingenieur drückt (auf) die Taste.
Contrary to German, in composed verbs (zusammengesetzte Verben, or: Prädikate), the object must also be placed after the verb.
The engineer has bought a book.
He is reading it.
I am going to read it, too.
In contrast to German, the word order is not changed when an adverb initiates the sentence.
Now we are working on the laser gauging equipment. In the design department I met Mr. Riggs.
Fortunately, I hadn't forgotten the formula.
There is also no change in the word order when the sentence comprises a conjunctional subordinate clause (konjunktionaler Nebensatz) and an added principle clause (nachgestellter Hauptsatz).
As soon as I have done my work, I will have a cup of tea.

### Exercises

Form sentences in the correct word order.
Subjects: designer, section leader.
Verbs: operate, telephone.
Objects: design office, turning lathe.
Adverbs: now, tomorrow.

*sentence structure* Satz(auf)bau - *word order* Wortfolge - *rigid(ly)* starr, steif - *to press* drükken - *key* Taste - *contrary to* im Gegensatz zu - *to place* setzen, anordnen - *in contrast to* im Gegensatz zu - *to initiate* einleiten, beginnen - *gauging* Mess . . . - *equipment* Gerät(e), Anlage(n), Ausrüstung - *design department* Konstruktionsbüro - *fortunately* glücklicherweise - *to comprise* umfassen - *designer* Konstrukteur - *section leader* Gruppenleiter - *to operate* arbeiten, bedienen, betreiben - *turning lathe* Drehmaschine, Drehbank

## Unit 5.2

### Bedplate and frames of a marine diesel engine*

The bedplates and frames for the largest Fiat engines are normally built as a steel structure, with the inclusion of cast steel elements. A cast-iron construction is adopted for the smaller engine types. The bedplate consists of sections that are strongly bolted together. The aftermost section is connected to the thrust-block section, thus providing great rigidity and ensuring complete and easy alignment. The thrust block is lubricated with oil directly drawn from the general lubricating system. The transverse girders of the bedplate contain the main bearing

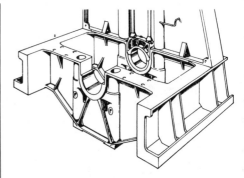

Bedplate and frame of a diesel engine.

housings. These are all machined together for obtaining perfect crankshaft alignment. The A frames are mounted on the bedplate and support the cylinders. The A frames on one side of the engine are connected to each other by the crosshead guides and, on the other, by simple strut elements. The openings between the frames are closed by large access doors.

*bedplate* Grundplatte - *frame* Ständer - *marine diesel engine* Schiffsdieselmotor - *built* (to build) gebaut - *structure* Konstruktion, Aufbau, Bauart - *inclusion* Aufnahme, Einschluss - *cast steel* Gussstahl - *construction* Aufbau; sonst auch: Bau - *to adopt* hier: verwenden; sonst: annehmen, adoptieren - *to consist of* bestehen aus - *section* Abschnitt, Sektion - *to bolt together* zusammenschrauben - *aftermost* hinterst - *to connect to* verbinden mit; sonst auch: anschliessen an - *thrust-block* Drucklager; sonst auch: Querstück - *to provide* sichern, vorsehen; sonst auch: liefern - *rigidity* Festigkeit, Steifheit - *to ensure* sichern, gewährleisten - *alignment* Ausrichtung, Fluchtung - *to lubricate* schmieren - *to draw* entnehmen; sonst auch: (ent)ziehen - *lubricating system* Schmieranlage, -system - *transverse girder* Bindequerträger -
*to contain* enthalten, aufnehmen - *main bearing housing* Kurbelwellenlagerstuhl - *to machine together* zusammen (d.h. gleichzeitig) maschinell bearbeiten - *to obtain* erhalten - *crankshaft* Kurbelwelle - *to mount* aufbauen, vorsehen, montieren - *to support* verstärken, (ab)stützen - *to connect to each other* gegenseitig verbinden - *crosshead guide* Kreuzkopfführung - *strut* Strebe, Versteifung - *access door* Zugangsklappe, -öffnung

## Verbs used in the description

*adopt* hier: verwenden; sonst: annehmen; in diesem Fall auch: use
*bolt together* zusammenschrauben
*build* (auf)bauen
*connect to* verbinden mit; hier auch: fix to
*consist of* bestehen aus; hier auch: build up of
*contain* enthalten, aufnehmen
*draw* entnehmen; hier auch: supply
*ensure* sichern, gewährleisten; hier auch: assure
*mount* aufbauen, vorsehen, montieren, hier auch: assemble
*obtain* erhalten
*provide* sichern, vorsehen, liefern
*support* verstärken, (ab)stützen; hier auch: carry

# Unit 5.3

## Help required to perform a task*

*I badly need two more designers to help me with the Bayswater contract.*
Ich benötige dringend noch zwei Konstrukteure zur Mitarbeit am Bayswater-Auftrag.
*Has Henry got enough people working with him?*
Hat Henry genug Leute zu seiner Unterstützung?
*Our section must have another draughtsman.*
Unsere Gruppe braucht noch einen Konstrukteur.
*How long will it take your draughtsman to design the key plans for the Bahia project?*
Wie lange brauchen eure Konstrukteure, um die Schlüsselpläne für das Bahia-Projekt zu zeichnen?
*How are you getting on with the MSE contract?*
Wie kommst du mit dem MSE-Auftrag voran?
*Who would be able to help me with this tricky system?*
Wer könnte (oder: ist in der Lage) mir bei diesem kniffligen System zu helfen?
*Please help me check the types and settings of the valves.*
Hilf mir bitte die Typen und Einstellungen der Ventile zu überprüfen.
*We must start work on the schematic diagrams by Wednesday at the latest.*
Wir müssen spätestens am Mittwoch mit der Arbeit an den Schemata beginnen.
*Would you please go and pick up the equipment to be arranged on the XY rack.*
Würdest du bitte die Geräte für das XY-Gestell holen.
*I'm looking for the chief test engineer. He'll have to give me a more detailed explanation about the regulator data.*
Ich suche den Prüffeldleiter. Er sollte mir eine ausführlichere Erklärung zu den Reglerdaten geben.

# Unit 5.4

## Providing of equipment

The electronic work simulator, shown on this picture, is a «Ministry of Progress» design.

The work simulator is equipped (or: fitted, furnished, provided) with various control devices and switches; e.g.:

*change-over switch* Umschalter
*control lever* Bedienungshebel, Steuerungshebel
*control valve* Steuerventil, Regelventil
*controller* Steuerschalter, Kontroller
*emergency switch* Not(aus)schalter
*illuminated push-button* Leuchtdruckknopf, Leuchttaste

*key* Taste, Druckknopf
*lighted push-button* Leuchtdruckknopf, Leuchttaste
*limit switch* Endschalter
*master key* Haupttaste
*lever key* Kippschalter
*push-button* Druckknopf, Drucktaste
*relay* Relais
*selector switch* Wahlschalter
*spring-loaded switch* Tastschalter
*toggle switch* Kippschalter
*control bay* Steuerfeld
*control box* Steuerkasten, Steuertafel
*control console* (US) Steuerpult
*control desk* Steuerpult
*control panel* Steuertafel
*distribution panel* Verteilertafel
*emergency switchboard* Notschalttafel
*key board* Tastatur, Tastenfeld
*switchboard* Schalttafel
*circuit-breaker* Leistungsschalter
*contactor* Schütz, Schaltschütz
*disconnector* Trenner
*disconnecting switch* Trennschalter
*fuse switch* Sicherungsschalter
*heavy-duty circuit-breaker* Leistungsschalter für schweren Schaltbetrieb
*isolating switch* Trennschalter
*isolator* Trenner
*lever switch* Hebelschalter
*master switch* Hauptschalter, Meisterschalter
*moulded-case circuit-breaker* gekapselter Leistungsschalter
*plug-in circuit-breaker* Einsteck-Leistungsschalter
*switchgear* Schaltgerät(e), Schaltanlage(n)

**That's the trouble nowadays – no knowledge of the classics!**

# Lesson 6

## Unit 6.1

### Present tenses, simple and continuous

There are two present tenses in English:
1. The simple present - I work
2. The present continuous - I am working

The present continuous tense is formed with the present tense of the auxiliary verb «to be» and the present participle (the infinitive + ing):
I am working on the drilling machine
you are working on the drilling machine
he (the machinist, operator) is working on the drilling machine
we are working on the drilling machine
you are working on the drilling machine
they are working on the drilling machine

The negative is formed by putting «not» after the auxiliary: I am not operating the boring machine
The interrogating (Frageform) is formed by inverting the subject and auxiliary:
am I controlling the engine speed?

### The present continuous tense of the verb «to work»

Affirmative (bejahend) - I am working
Negative - I am not working
Interrogative - am I working?

### Exercises

Conjugate in the affirmative, negative and interrogative: to control the speed of the diesel engine.

*present tense* Gegenwart, Gegenwartsform - *simple* einfach - *continuous* Verlaufsform - *to form* bilden - *auxiliary verb* Hilfszeitwort - *present participle* Partizip präsens, Mittelwort der Gegenwart - *drilling machine* Bohrmaschine - *to operate* arbeiten an, betreiben - *boring machine* Aufbohrmaschine - *to invert* umkehren - *to control* regulieren, steuern - *engine speed* Motordrehzahl

## Unit 6.2

### Checking the oil flow*

With superheated steam, the turbine journal attains a high temperature by heat conduction alone. A good flow of oil is required to keep the temperature from rising.
A small cock is fitted in the top of the bearing cover to provide a means of checking the oil flow or to allow air to escape when starting up. The bent pipe attached to it discharges oil into the funnel. It is also useful for drawing off samples for testing the condition of the oil.

*oil flow* Ölfluss - *superheated steam* überhitzter Dampf, Heissdampf - *journal* Wellenzapfen - *to attain* erreichen, erlangen - *heat conduction* Wärme(ab)leitung - *required* erforderlich - *to keep from rising* vor dem Anstieg (oder: Anstei-

gen) bewahren - *cock* Hahn(ventil) - *to fit* einbauen, einsetzen - *in the top* im obersten Teil -

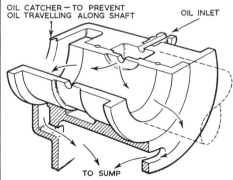

Path of oil in a turbine journal bearing.

*bearing cover* Lagerdeckel - *to provide* vorsehen - *means* (Hilfs-) Mittel, Möglichkeit - *to escape* entweichen, entkommen - *bent pipe* gebogenes (oder: gekrümmtes) Rohr - *to attach* anschliessen, anbauen - *to discharge* abfliessen; sonst auch: entladen - *funnel* Trichter; sonst auch: Schornstein - *to draw off* entnehmen - *samples* Proben - *condition* Zustand; sonst auch: Bedingungen

**Verbs used in the description**
*attach* anschliessen, anbauen
*attain* erreichen, erlangen; hier auch: achieve, reach
*check* überwachen; hier auch: examine
*discharge* abfliessen, entladen
*draw off* entnehmen; hier auch: obtain
*escape* entweichen, entkommen; hier auch: release
*fit* einbauen, einsetzen; hier auch: provide
*keep from* bewahren vor; hier auch: prevent
*provide* vorsehen

## Unit 6.3

### Replacing bearing bushes*

Bearing bushes are easily removed when the weight of the rotor is taken up. The turbine rotor, with its journal, needs to be lifted only a few thousandths of an inch to enable the bottom half to be pushed round the shaft and lifted out. This can be done without disturbing the sealing glands.

*to replace* ersetzen, auswechseln - *bearing bush* Lagerschale - *to remove* entfernen, ausbauen - *weight* Gewicht - *to take up* aufnehmen - *to lift* (an)heben - *inch* Zoll - *to enable* ermöglichen, in den Stand setzen - *bottom half* untere Hälfte - *to push round* herumdrücken, herumschieben -

*shaft* Welle - *to disturb* beeinträchtigen, stören - *sealing gland* Stopfbuchsendichtung

**Verbs used in the description**
*disturb* beeinträchtigen, stören; hier auch: interfere with
*enable* ermöglichen, in den Stand setzen
*lift* (an)heben; hier auch: raise
*lift out* herausheben; hier auch: take out, lift clear
*push round* herumdrücken, herumschieben; hier auch: turn round
*remove* entfernen; hier auch: take out
*replace* ersetzen, auswechseln; hier auch: renew

## Unit 6.4

### Erecting engineers replace bearing bushes

*First of all, the bearing cover must be removed.*
(Or: The first thing to do is to remove the bearing cover.)
Als erstes muss der Lagerdeckel abgenommen (oder: abgebaut) werden.

*Please hand me the ring spanner.*
Reich mir bitte den Ringschlüssel.

*The bolts are very tight.*
Die Schrauben sitzen sehr fest.

*Careful, we are taking off the cover.*
Vorsicht, wir heben jetzt den Deckel ab.

*Now starts the most difficult job.*
Wir gehen jetzt an die schwierigste Arbeit (heran).

*The turbine rotor, with its journal, must be lifted (or: raised).*
Der Turbinenrotor, mit seinem Wellenzapfen, muss angehoben werden.

*A few thousandths of an inch will do.*
Einige Tausendstel Zoll reichen aus.

*Now push the bottom bearing bush around the shaft.*

Schiebe jetzt die untere Lagerschale um die Welle.
*That went well. Just secure the shaft over there.*
Das ging gut. Sichere doch die Welle dort hinten.
*The new bearing bush can now be inserted without difficulty.*

Die neue Lagerschale kann nun leicht eingesetzt werden.
*But aligning the shaft will still take us some time.*
(Or: It will take us some time to align the shaft.)
Es wird aber noch einige Zeit dauern, bis wir die Welle ausgerichtet haben.

# Unit 6.5

## Technical periodical

### Enquiry

Dear Sirs,
I am considering subscribing to your periodical «Engineering Report» and would be pleased if you would let me know the respective costs of a 6-monthly and yearly subscription, including air-mail postage to Switzerland. Please also advise how payment should be made.
Yours faithfully,
Urs Eggenberger
CH-9403 Goldach

### Subscription

I should like to take out a six months' subscription for your periodical «Engineering Report» and have instructed my bank to transfer £ 60 to cover the cost.

### Renewing subscription

Would you please renew my subscription for your periodical «Engineering Report» for a further year when my present one expires on 31st May. I enclose a cheque for £ 120.

*periodical* Zeitschrift - *enquiry* Erkundigung, Nachfrage, Anfrage - *to consider* erwägen, (sich) überlegen - *to subscribe (to)* abonnieren, bestellen - *subscription* Abonnement - *including* einschliesslich - *air-mail postage* Gebühr für Luftpostzustellung - *to advise* angeben, beraten - *to take out* abonnieren - *to instruct* anweisen - *to transfer* überweisen - *to cover* decken - *to renew* erneuern - *present* jetzig, momentan - *to expire* ablaufen, enden, verfallen - *to enclose* einschliessen, beifügen

"I can't give you a pay rise, but if you once should need an interceptor, I'll give you a rebate of 20 per cent."
"Ich kann Ihnen keine Gehaltszulage geben, aber wenn sie einmal einen Abfangjäger brauchen, gebe ich Ihnen 20 Prozent Rabatt."

# Lesson 7

## Unit 7.1

### The past and perfect tenses
#### The simple past tense
The simple past tense in regular verbs is formed by adding -ed to the infinitive. Infinitive: to work; simple past: worked. The negative of regular and irregular verbs is formed with «did not» and the infinitive (without «to»). I did not work, you did not work, etc.
Affirmative (bejahend): I worked
Negative: I did not work
Interrogative (Frageform): did I work?
Negative interrogative: did I not work?

#### Exercises
I operated the radio set
you operated the radio set

Write also in the negative, interrogative and negative interrogative.

#### The past continuous tense
The past continuous tense is formed by the past tense of the verb «to be» + the present participle (Partizip).
Affirmative (bejahend): I was working
Negative: I was not working
Interrogative (Frageform): was I working?

#### Exercises
I was starting the pump motor
you were starting the pump motor

Write also in the negative and interrogative.

#### The present perfect tense
The present perfect tense is formed with the present tense of «to have» + the past participle.
Affirmative: I have worked
Negative: I have not worked
Interrogative: have I worked?
Negative interrogative: have I not worked?

#### Exercises
I have aligned the coupling
you have aligned the coupling

Write also in other forms.

#### Some odd present perfect examples
*The electrical erector has switched on the motor.*
Der Elektromonteur hat den Motor eingeschaltet.

*The designer has inserted the circuit card.*
Der Konstrukteur hat die Leiterplatte eingesetzt.

*The electrician has disconnected the power supply cable.*
Der Elektriker hat das Speisekabel herausgezogen (oder: abgeklemmt).

*I have shut down the system (or: plant).*
Ich habe die Anlage abgestellt.

*I have started up the forced draught fan.*
Ich habe das (Kessel-)Gebläse angefahren (oder: angelassen, gestartet).

*I have commissioned the steam plant.*
Ich habe die Dampfanlage in Betrieb gesetzt (oder: übergeben).

## Unit 7.2

### Cylinder liner of a marine diesel engine *

The figure shows a cylinder liner, with exhaust and scavenging ports, in a cylinder block. The water space is sealed by means of a stuffing-box, with a leakage groove underneath. In the event of leakage, the water is visibly discharged through this groove. Liners are made of cast iron alloy, the wearing properties of which have been proven for many years. In the middle of the cylinder, at the manœuvring side, an inspection hole is provided through which the piston can be inspected when the engine is shut down. Inspection holes enable exhaust ports to be cleaned, when the pistons are at B.D.C., with a special tool which is combined with a kind of soot-blower. For smaller engines the liner is in one piece, inserted from the top of the cylinder block. The larger engines have mostly two-piece liners, the lower part being inserted from the bottom end of the cylinder block and fastened to it by a flange. Sometimes, a one-piece liner design is also used for the larger engine types. Both designs have their advantages as regards manufacturing and servicing of the engine.

*cylinder liner* Zylinderlaufbüchse - *marine diesel engine* Schiffsdieselmotor - *exhaust port* Auspuffkanal, Austrittsöffnung - *scavenging port* Spülschlitz, Spülluftkanal - *water space* Wasserraum - *to seal* abschliessen, abdichten - *by means of* mittels - *stuffing-box* Stopfbüchse - *leakage groove* Lecknut - *underneath* darunter - *in the event of* im Falle, falls - *visible (-bly)* sichtbar - *to discharge* (aus)laufen; sonst auch: entladen - *cast iron alloy* Gusseisenlegierung - *wearing property* Laufeigenschaft, Verschleisseigenschaft - *proven* bewährt - *manœvring side* Manövrierseite (Steuerstand) - *inspection hole* Schauloch - *to provide* vorsehen - *piston* Kolben - *to shut down* abstellen - *to enable* ermöglichen, in den Stand setzen - *B.D.C.* bottom dead centre: unterer Totpunkt - *tool* Werkzeug - *kind* Art - *soot-blower* Russbläser - *one-piece* in einem Stück - *to insert* einsetzen - *from the top* von oben - *lower part* unterer Teil - *to fasten* befestigen - *flange* Flansch - *design* Ausführung, Konstruktion - *advantage* Vorteil - *as regards* hinsichtlich, was betrifft - *manufacturing* Herstellung - *servicing* Wartung (manchmal auch: Bedienung)

### Verbs used in the description

*discharge* (aus)fliessen; hier auch: let out, run out, emit
*enable* ermöglichen, in den Stand setzen; hier auch: permit
*fasten* befestigen; hier auch: secure, fix
*insert* einsetzen; hier auch: fit, assemble
*inspect* inspizieren, prüfen; hier auch: examine
*provide* vorsehen; hier auch: foresee
*seal* abschliessen, abdichten; hier auch: segregate, separate
*shut down* abstellen, abgestellt; hier auch: out of operation, at standstill

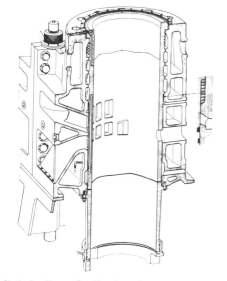

Cylinder liner of a diesel engine

# Unit 7.3

## Starting a centrifugal pump*

A centrifugal feed pump must not be operated unless it is filled with water. This is called priming. The pump casing, the suction pipe and the discharge pipe up to the check valve must be completely filled. If the water enters the pump suction pipe by gravity, priming is not necessary and the pump will remain full of water when shut down. To fill the pump, open the smaller air-valve on the top of the pump casing until water commences to flow from it, then shut.

If the pump is operated with a suction lift, it may be primed either from an independent water supply or from the discharge line, or by means of a vent connection which will evacuate the pump and suction piping of air. The check valve must, of course, be fitted in these cases. The discharge valve and air-valves should be kept closed during the priming of the pump if the latter methods are used. To start the centrifugal pump, proceed as follows: Check lubrication, and see that pump glands are properly packed and adjusted. Open steam and exhaust casing drain cocks of the driving engine; open steam and exhaust valves; open suction valves and air-cocks. Open turbine throttle valve sufficiently to free the pipelines, steam chest and exhaust casing of water while running turbine at a very low speed. When free of water, close the drain cocks and bring the unit up to speed.

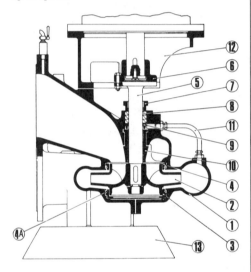

Captions in the pump drawing
1  *pump casing and cover* Pumpengehäuse und Gehäusedeckel
2  *impeller* Laufrad
3  *casing ring (bottom)* Gehäusering (unten)
4  *casing ring (top)* Gehäusering (oben)
4A *locking pins* Sperringe, Spannringe
5  *pump shaft* Pumpenwelle
6  *coupling (motor half)* Kupplung (Motorhälfte)
7  *gland* Stopfbuchse
8  *packing* Packung
9  *lantern ring (split)* Laternenring (zweiteilig, geschnitten)
10 *neck bush* Halsbuchse
11 *water service pipe to stuffing box* Kontrollrohr zur Stopfbuchse
12 *motor support* Motoruntersatz, Motorbock
13 *pump foot* Pumpenfuss

*centrifugal pump* Kreiselpumpe - *must not* hier: darf nicht - *to operate* betreiben, arbeiten - *priming* Anfüllen - *casing* Gehäuse - *suction pipe* Saugleitung, Ansaugrohr - *pipe branch* Zweigleitung, Abzweigrohr - *discharge stop valve* Druckabsperrventil - *to enter* einlaufen, eintreten - *gravity* Gefälle; sonst auch: Schwere, Schwerkraft - *to prime* anfüllen - *necessary* notwendig - *to remain* bleiben - *to shut down* abstellen - *air-valve* Luftventil - *on the top* oben auf - *to commence* beginnen - *to flow* fliessen, strömen - *to shut* schliessen - *suction lift* Saughöhe - *independent* unabhängig - *supply* Zufluss; sonst auch: Lieferung, Versorgung - *discharge line* Entlastungsleitung - *by means of* mittels - *vent connection* Entlüftungsanschluss - *to evacuate* entlüften, evakuieren - *check valve* Absperrventil - *to fit* einbauen, einsetzen - *case* Fall - *latter* letztere - *to proceed* vorgehen - *lubrication* Schmierung - *gland* Stopfbuchse - *properly* ordnungsgemäss - *to pack* abdichten, verpacken - *to adjust* einstellen, ausrichten - *exhaust* Ausgangs . . ., Austritts . . . - *drain cock* Entleerungshahn - *driving engine* Antriebsmaschine - *throttle valve* Drosselventil, Reglerventil - *sufficient(ly)* ausreichend - *steam chest* Ventilkasten - *speed* Drehzahl - *to bring up to speed* hochfahren (auf Nenndrehzahl)

### Verbs used in the description

*adjust* einstellen, ausrichten; hier auch: align, insert
*bring up to speed* hochfahren; hier auch: speed up
*commence* beginnen; hier auch: start
*enter* einlaufen, eintreten; hier auch: flow into
*evacuate* entlüften, evakuieren; hier auch: remove the air
*fit* einbauen, einsetzen; hier auch: provide
*operate* betreiben, arbeiten; hier auch: put into operation, commission
*prime* anfüllen
*proceed as follows* es ist vorzugehen wie folgt; hier auch: the following steps should be taken
*shut* schliessen; hier auch: close
*shut down* abstellen; hier auch: put out of operation, stop

# Unit 7.4

## On the telephone*

Good morning. My name is Keller, Bodmer & Frei Company, speaking from Goldach, Switzerland.
Guten Morgen. Mein Name ist Keller, Firma B. & F., in Goldach in der Schweiz.

*I should like to speak to Mr. White.*
Ich möchte gern mit Mr. White sprechen.

*Just a moment, I'll see if Mr. White is available.*
Einen Moment, ich werde mal nachsehen, ob Mr. White frei ist.

*Mr. White, a Mr. Brugger is on the line for you.*
Mr. White, ein Herr Brugger möchte Sie am Telefon sprechen.

*Put him through, please.*
Stellen Sie ihn bitte durch.

*I'll transfer you to Mr. White now.*
Ich werde Sie jetzt zu Mr. White durchstellen.

*The connection is very bad. I can hardly understand you.*
Die Verbindung ist sehr schlecht. Ich kann Sie kaum verstehen.

*Please hang up. I'll ring you again immediately. I hope the connection will be better then.*
Legen Sie bitte den Hörer auf. Ich rufe Sie gleich wieder an. Vielleicht ist die Verbindung dann besser.

*Hold the line please.*
Bleiben Sie bitte am Apparat.

*Mr. White is at a meeting. Can he ring you up later, say about 11 o'clock. I hope he'll be back by then.*
Mr. White ist an einer Besprechung. Kann er Sie später anrufen, sagen wir um 11 Uhr. Ich hoffe, dass er bis dahin zurück ist.

*What time shall I ring you tomorrow?*
Um welche Zeit soll ich Sie morgen anrufen?

*Please give me Mr. White again.*
Geben Sie mir bitte noch einmal Mr. White.

*Biggs and Walker here, my name is Baker. I'd like to speak to Mr. Hunter.*
Hier ist Biggs und Walker, mein Name ist Baker. Ich möchte gern mit Herrn Hunter sprechen.

*Am I speaking to the chief test engineer?*
Spreche ich mit dem Prüffeld-Leiter?

*Would you please repeat that.*
Würden Sie das bitte wiederholen.

*Speak up please.*
Sprechen Sie bitte lauter.

*I'm sorry, but I didn't catch your name.*
Es tut mir leid, aber ich habe Ihren Namen nicht verstanden.

*Please give my regards to Mr. Wilson.*
Bestellen Sie bitte Mr. Wilson einen schönen Gruss.

*Goodbye Mr. Cox. Thanks for calling.*
Auf Wiedersehen Mr. Cox. Vielen Dank für den Anruf.

# Unit 7.5

## Watch the magnet for better ignition timing

A novel method of adjusting a car's spark plug timing relative to camshaft position is suggested by Ford in BP 1328945. Well-adjusted timing means that cars perform more efficiently and their exhaust gases are cleaner.
Until now timing checks have been made with an inspection hatch removed from the crankcase and with the engine stationary or running and lit by neon flashes powered by the spark coil. But such adjustment can be tricky, especially in bright sunlight which swamps the neon flashes.
Ford's idea is that the crankshaft should have a small projection which either houses a magnet or is itself magnetised. At a point along the path of the projection, a hole is bored through the engine crankcase and filled with a plug of non-ferrous material. The plug houses an electromagnetic transducer which produces a sharply

peaked output signal every time the magnetic projection passes. The output signal from the transducer indicates a reference position and the distributor can then be adjusted to a position designed for accurate ignition timing. The output of the transducer could also probably be used to feed an electronic device for comparing ignition with crankshaft location during engine running.

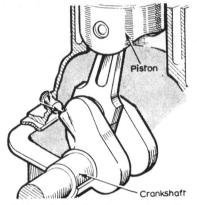

The timing device is connected to the plug shown left in the middle of the sketch.

*ignition timing* Zünd(zeit)punkteinstellung - *novel* neuartig - *to adjust* einstellen, nachstellen - *spark plug* Zündkerze - *relative to* entsprechend der . . .; sonst auch: bezüglich - *camshaft position* Stellung der Nockenwelle - *to suggest* vorschlagen - *to perform more efficiently* mehr Leistung abgeben - *exhaust gas* Abgas - *timing check* Prüfung des Zündzeitpunktes - *inspection hatch* Beobachtungsöffnung - *to remove* entfernen - *crankcase* Kurbelgehäuse - *stationary* (fest)stehend - *lit* (to light) (ange)leuchtet - *flash* Blitz - *powered by* betrieben durch - *spark coil* Zündspule - *adjustment* Einstellung - *tricky* heikel, knifflig - *to swamp* überdecken; sonst auch: überschwemmen - *projection* hier: Anbau - *to house* aufnehmen - *path* Bahn, Pfad - *to bore* (auf)bohren - *plug* Verschlussschraube - *non-ferrous* Nichteisen... - *transducer* (Energie-)Wandler - *to produce* erzeugen - *sharply peaked output signal* spitzes (kurzes) Ausgangssignal - *to pass* passieren - *to indicate* anzeigen - *distributor* Verteiler - *to design* abstimmen; sonst auch: entwerfen, konstruieren - *to feed* speisen - *device* Gerät, Vorrichtung - *crankshaft location* Stellung der Kurbelwelle

**Ministry of Progress: "The new economic report will be released soon."**

# Lesson 8

# Unit 8.1

## The future

The future tense in English is shall/will with the infinitive, without «to»:
I shall (or: will) go, he will go etc.
However, this is not the only way of expressing the future. The following methods are possible, each being used in a slighly different way.

1. *The simple present*
   Das einfache Präsens
   *We leave at six o'clock and arrive in London at eight o'clock.*
   Wir fahren um sechs Uhr los und kommen um acht Uhr in London an.
2. *The present continuous*
   Die Verlaufsform des Präsens
   *He ist testing the equipment tonight.*
   Er prüft die Geräte (oder: Anlage) heute abend (oder: heute nacht).
3. *The «going to»form*
   Die «going to»-Umschreibung
   *He is going to change the system.*
   Er wird die Anlage (oder: das System) ändern.
4. *The future tense*
   Das Futurum (1. Futur)
   *You'll have time to inspect the workshops.*
   Sie werden Zeit (genug) haben, die Werkstätten zu besichtigen.
5. *The future continuous*
   Die Verlaufsform des Futurs
   *I'm seeing the designer tomorrow.*
   Ich sehe den Konstrukteur morgen.
6. *The future perfect tense*
   Das Futurum exactum (2. Futur)
   *By two years time, the equipment will have been replaced.*
   Innerhalb von zwei Jahren (oder: in zwei Jahren) werden die Geräte ausgewechselt (sein).

## Note on the «going to» form

Actions expressed by the «going to» form are usually considered very likely to be performed. This form can be used for the near future with a time expression as an alternative to the present continuous, because when the «going to» form is used with a definite time, the action which it expresses becomes very definite and there is then very little difference between the two future forms: I am meeting the chief test engineer at the test station at six o'clock. – I am going to meet the chief test engineer at the test station at six o'clock.

## Exercises

Work out conjugations
in the future tense and «going to» form:
I'll read off the ammeter
you'll read off the ammeter
he'll (the designer will) read

I'm going to read off the ammeter
you're going to read off the ammeter

## Other examples:

I'll take a reading from the voltmeter.
I'll adjust the potentiometer.
I'll reset limit switch b9.
I'll depress the stop button.
I'll pull out the power plug.
I'll put the fan into operation.
I'll operate the vertical mill.
I'll investigate the noise problem.
I'll strip down the controller.
I'll commission the Trowbridge scheme.
I'll remove the bearing cover.
I'll align the coupling.
I'll look into the noise problem.

# Unit 8.2

## Carbon glands for marine turbines*

Some sort of packing must be provided where the rotor shaft or spindle passes through the turbine casing, just as the piston-rod of a reciprocating steam engine requires packing to prevent steam escaping at the H.P. end, and to prevent air being drawn in at the L.P. end.

An ordinary stuffing-box and gland with soft steam packing would seal the space between the casing and the shaft, but the packing would wear away the surface of the shaft and there would also be friction losses.

Temperature changes would cause expansion and contraction, sufficient to cause leakage, and this leakage would be most undesirable at the L.P. end. The leakage at the L.P. end is, of course, from the atmosphere into the turbine, due to the pressure inside the turbine being lower than atmospheric pressure. When the normal vacuum is very high it only requires a small opening for leakage of air to make it impossible for the air-pump to cope with it, with the result that the vacuum drops. A drop in vacuum in a turbine installation results in loss of power and efficiency. A reduction of 1 in. in vacuum, from 29 in. to 28 in., results in about five per cent loss of power. In turbines the glands may consists of two rings of a carbon composite material at each end. The rings are of square section and in halves, with a garter holding them firmly together and pressing them lightly onto the surface of the shaft. This is called a carbon gland. An approximate rule for carbon packing is that its inner surface should be 0.001 in. clear of the shaft surface when cold for every 1 in. of the diameter.

*carbon gland* Kohlestopfbuchse; carbon auch: Kohlenstoff - *packing* Packung, Packmaterial, Dichtung - *to provide* vorsehen - *shaft* Welle - *to pass through* führen durch - *casing* Gehäuse - *piston-rod* Kolbenstange: bei Verbrennungsmotoren auch: Pleuel - *reciprocating steam engine* Dampfkolbenmaschine; reciprocating auch: hin- und hergehend - *to require* erfordern - *to prevent* verhindern - *to escape* entweichen, entkommen - *H.P.* high-pressure: Hochdruck... - *end* hier: Seite - *to draw in* einziehen - *L.P.* low-pressure: Niederdruck ...
*ordinary* gewöhnlich, einfach - *stuffing-box* Stopfbüchse (allgemein) - *soft* weich - *to seal* abdichten - *space* Raum - *to wear away* verschleissen, abarbeiten - *surface* Oberfläche - *friction losses* Reibungsverluste - *to cause* verursachen, bewirken - *expansion* Ausdehnung, Dehnung - *contraction* Zusammenziehung, Schrumpfung - *sufficient* ausreichend - *leakage* Undichtheit, Verlust; sonst auch: Leck(en), Abfliessen - *due to* wegen, zurückzuführen auf - *opening* Öffnung - *air-pump* Luftpumpe - *to cope with* fertigwerden mit - *result* Resultat - *to drop* fallen, abfallen - *drop* Abfallen, Abfall - *installation* hier: Anlage - *to result in* zur Folge haben - *loss of power* Leistungsverlust - *efficiency* Wirkungsgrad; sonst auch: Wirksamkeit, Tüchtigkeit - *in.* inch: Zoll - *to consist of* bestehen aus - *carbon composite* Kohlezusammensetzung (oder: Kohlenstoffzusammensetzung) - *square* quadratisch - *section* Querschnitt - *garter* Ringband - *firm(ly)* fest - *to press* drücken - *approximate* ungefähr - *rule* Regel - *diameter* Durchmesser

### Verbs used in the description

*cause* verursachen, bewirken; hier auch: result in
*cope with* fertigwerden mit; hier auch: make good the loss
*draw in* einziehen; hier auch: come in
*drop* fallen, abfallen; hier auch: fall
*escape* entweichen, entkommen; hier auch: come out
*hold* halten; hier auch: keep
*pass through* führen durch; hier auch: go through

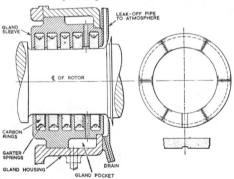

Carbon gland of a marine turbine.

*press* drücken; hier auch: exercise pressure
*prevent* verhindern; hier auch: stop
*provide* vorsehen; hier auch: use, employ
*require* erfordern; hier auch: need

*result in* zur Folge haben; hier auch: mean
*seal* abdichten; hier auch: close
*wear away* verschleissen, abarbeiten; hier auch: grind

# Unit 8.3

## Mounting equipment
### Verbs used for mounting equipment
*accommodate* unterbringen, aufnehmen
*affix* anhängen, anbringen
*apply* anwenden, auftragen, eintragen, anlegen (Spannung)
*arrange* anordnen, aufstellen, beiordnen, einrichten
*assemble* zusammenbauen, zusammensetzen, montieren, einbauen
*attach* anbauen, befestigen, anbringen, aufsetzen, anhängen, vorsetzen
*bolt* verschrauben, festschrauben, anschrauben, befestigen, verbolzen
*build* bauen, aufbauen, errichten
*encapsulate* einkapseln, kapseln, einhülsen
*enclose* einschliessen, umgrenzen, einkapseln, kapseln
*equip* ausrüsten, ausstatten, einrichten, versehen (mit)
*erect* errichten, aufbauen, aufrichten, montieren, setzen
*fasten* befestigen, festmachen
*fit* einpassen, zusammenpassen, versehen, passen, anbringen, montieren
*fix* anbringen, befestigen, festmachen, einsetzen, aufspannen
*house* unterbringen, aufnehmen, einbauen
*incorporate* einbauen, unterbringen
*insert* einsetzen, aufstecken, einstecken, einlegen
*install* installieren, einbauen, montieren, errichten, aufstellen
*lay* legen, verlegen
*locate* plazieren, anordnen, in Stellung bringen
*mount* montieren, aufstellen, zusammensetzen, einbauen
*place* anordnen, plazieren, verlegen, auflegen
*provide* vorsehen, liefern, sorgen für
*screw* schrauben, festschrauben, verschrauben
*set* setzen, einrichten, einstellen, anziehen

*The battery charger and panel are to be installed in the emergency diesel generator room.*
Das Batterieladegerät mit der Ladetafel sind im Notdiesel(generator)raum aufzustellen.

*Control cabinets should be located in easily accessible positions.*
Steuerschränke sollten an gut zugänglichen Stellen untergebracht werden.

*Where steam and oil gauges are mounted on the main propulsion console, care is to be taken that the steam or oil cannot come into contact with the energised parts.*
Wo Dampf- und Ölmanometer in das Hauptfahrpult eingebaut werden, ist dafür Sorge zu tragen, dass Dampf oder Öl nicht in Kontakt mit spannungsführenden Teilen kommen kann.

*A warning sign must be affixed to the unit housing warning the operator of the presence of high voltage within.*
Ein Warnschild ist auf dem Geräteschrank anzubringen, das den Bedienungsmann (oder das Personal) davon in Kenntnis setzt, dass Hochspannung im Schrank ist.

*This equipment may even be fitted where space is at premium.*
Diese Geräte können selbst dort angebracht werden, wo der Platz äusserst knapp bemessen ist.

*Foundation bolts that are to be embedded in concrete must not be painted.*
Fundamentschrauben, die in Beton eingelassen werden, dürfen nicht angestrichen werden.

*Each switchboard must be completely assembled at the factory and tested by the manufacturer.*
Jede Schalttafel ist in der Fabrik vollständig zusammenzubauen und vom Hersteller zu prüfen.

*The secondary windings of the current transformers must be earthed at the panel which houses the associated relays.*
Die Sekundärwicklungen der Stromwandler müssen bei der Tafel geerdet werden, welche die dazugehörigen Relais aufnimmt.

## Zeitwörter, die für Montieren und Einbauen von Geräten verwendet werden

| | | |
|---|---|---|
| anbauen | einbauen | montieren |
| anbringen | einbetten | plazieren |
| anordnen | einfügen | schrauben |
| anschrauben | einlassen | setzen |
| aufnehmen | einlegen | unterbringen |
| aufsetzen | einpassen | verlegen |
| aufstellen | einsetzen | verschrauben |
| ausrüsten | einschliessen | versehen |
| ausstatten | errichten | vorsehen |
| befestigen | installieren | zusammenbauen |
| beiordnen | kapseln | zusammensetzen |

## Verbs used for removing and stripping equipment

| | | |
|---|---|---|
| detach | remove | unbolt |
| disconnect | strip | unfasten |
| dismantle | strip down | unscrew |
| | take apart | |
| | take off | |

## Zeitwörter, die für Abbauen und Auseinandernehmen von Geräten verwendet werden

| | | |
|---|---|---|
| abbauen | auseinander- | entfernen |
| abmontieren | nehmen | zerlegen |
| abnehmen | demontieren | |

### Please note
Do not use «demount» although this verb can be found in some dictionaries; though correct in the meaning «remove» or «disassemble» it should not be used in technical descriptions.

The verb «strip» is used for removing equipment or materials which will not be refitted at reassembly; e.g. the turbine lagging, pipe lagging, conductor insulation etc.
To «strip» a machine down means to disassemble it. All parts may be used in the reassembly.

## Frequency of verbs used in a turbine specification

The following list gives an idea of the significance of verbs used in a 5-page specification, comprising approximately 200 lines.

| | | |
|---|---|---|
| provide 12× | Those occuring 1×: | fix |
| arrange 5× | accomplish | house |
| exceed 5× | affix | incorporate |
| prevent 5× | apply | insert |
| consist (of) 4× | assemble | lay |
| fit 4× | attach | lead |
| locate 4× | bolt | lift |
| secure 4× | bond | line |
| contain 3× | build | limit |
| design 3× | connect | mount |
| include 3× | control | observe |
| machine 3× | construct | pass |
| obtain 3× | deliver | place |
| equip 2× | design | propose |
| install 2× | detect | recess |
| maintain 2× | dismantle | remove |
| permit 2× | enclose | repair |
| support 2× | facilitate | set |
| | fasten | screw |
| | finish | supply |
| | | test |
| | | use |

Total number of verbs: 60 | | withstand

"How about the room temperature now, Miss Forsyte?"
(Punch, London)

# Unit 8.4

Flow chart of a coal-fired power station

Betriebsablaufschema eines Kraftwerkes mit Kohlefeuerung

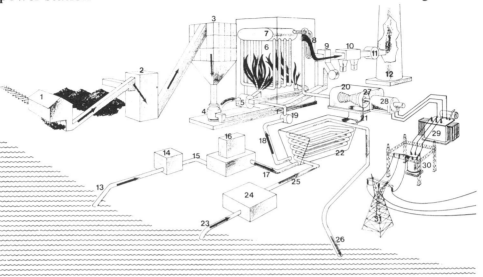

1 *unloading shed* Entladehalle
2 *coal crusher* Kohlenzerkleinerungsanlage; crusher sonst auch: Brecher
3 *coal bunker* Kohlenbunker
4 *pulverizer* Pulverisierer
5 *fuel injector* Brennstoffeinblasung
6 *combustion chamber* Verbrennungskammer
7 *boiler drum* Kesseltrommel
8 *superheater* Überhitzer
9 *air heater* Lufterhitzer
10 *dust collectors* Staubsammler
11 *induced draft fan* Saugzugventilator
12 *stack* Schornstein; sonst auch: Meiler, Stapel
13 *boiler water intake* Kesselwasserentnahme; intake sonst auch: Eintritt
14 *boiler water pumphouse* Kesselwasser-Pumphaus
15 *untreated water* unaufbereitetes Wasser
16 *water treatment building* Wasseraufbereitungsgebäude

17 *treated boiler water* aufbereitetes Kesselwasser
18 *boiler water feed line* Kesselwasserzuleitung
19 *boiler pump* Kesselpumpe
20 *high-pressure steam* Hochdruckdampf
21 *exhaust steam* Abdampf; exhaust sonst auch: Auspuff
22 *condenser* Kondensator
23 *cooling water intake* Kühlwasserentnahme
24 *cooling water pumphouse* Kühlwasser-Pumphaus
25 *condenser cooling water* Kondensatorkühlwasser
26 *cooling water return* Kühlwasserrücklauf
27 *steam turbine* Dampfturbine
28 *alternator* (Wechselstrom-)Generator
29 *transformer* Transformator
30 *circuit-breaker* Leistungsschalter
31 *transmission line tower* Hochspannungs-(übertragungs)mast

# Unit 8.5

## What a cracker *

Ultrasonic crack detectors are well established as a nondestructive method of testing materials but so far have always been thought of as lacking precision. But now a device has been developed by scientists at Harwell, which, under the most favourable conditions can measure the depth of cracks to an accuracy of 0.05 mm: this compares with the 3 mm accuracy obtainable by similar gauges.

The instrument works on the principle that ultrasound is passed between two probes held at a set distance either side of a crack and on the same surface. Sound waves would normally pass straight along the surface, but on encountering the crack they are diffracted down it and up the other side. The length of time a particular wave takes to travel between one probe and the other can be used to calculate the crack's depth. At Harwell, researchers have used the instrument to measure cracks one centimetre deep, with a normal operating accuracy of between 0.25 and 0.5 mm. Most similar gauges use ultrasound as well but work on the echo effect or the fact that the wave amplitude is proportional to crack depth, both methods being liable to error according to Harwell.

The prototype of the Harwell device displays time lag on a screen, figures being converted to give the crack depth.

*cracker* 1. tolle Sache, 2. Knallfrosch - *ultrasonic* Ultraschall - *crack* Riss, Sprung - *established* eingeführt - *non-destructive* zerstörungsfrei - *lacking* mangelnd, fehlend - *precision* Genauigkeit, Präzision - *device* Gerät - *to develop* entwickeln - *scientist* Wissenschafter - *favourable* günstig, vorteilhaft - *to measure* messen - *depth* Tiefe - *accuracy* Genauigkeit - *to compare with* vergleichen mit - *obtainable* erreichbar, möglich - *similar* ähnlich - *gauge* Messgerät - *ultrasound* Ultraschall - *to pass* leiten, senden - *probe* Sonde - *distance* Abstand, Entfernung - *surface* (Ober-)fläche - *soundwave* Schallwelle - *straight* direkt, gerade - *to encounter* (auf-)stossen, treffen - *to diffract* beugen - *length* Länge Dauer - *particular* einzeln - *to calculate* (er)rechnen - *researcher* Forscher - *echo effect* Echowirkung, -effekt - *to be liable to* anfällig sein auf, ausgesetzt sein - *error* Fehler - *according to* gemäss, nach - *to display* anzeigen - *time lag* Zeitverzögerung - *screen* Schirm - *figure* Zahl - *to convert* umwandeln, umrechnen

"Heavens, he's lit the filter again."

# Lesson 9

## Unit 9.1

### The participles

The present participle (Partizip präsens = Mittelwort der Gegenwart), infinite + ing, can be used as follows.

*As an adjective*
Running water, dripping taps.

*To form continuous tenses*
He is working. We are being followed.

*After verbs of sensation*
I smell something burning. I felt the house shaking.

*When one action is immediately followed by another by the same subject the first action can be expressed by a present participle. The participle must be placed first.*
Opening the drawer he took out a revolver.
(He opened the drawer and took out a revolver.)

*When the second action forms part of the first, or is a result of it we can express the second action by a present participle.*
The chief test engineer went out, slamming the door.

### Common participle examples

The erecting engineer was seen leaving the workshop at eleven o'clock.
We found the engineer in the power station adjusting the turbine regulator.
After visiting the works, we returned to New York.
Coming back from Mexico, I found two letters from the Power Authority.
After reading the letter, he showed signs of relief.
If sending a letter abroad, you should put a 80 Rappen stamp on it.
Sometimes people call up who have difficulty expressing themselves clearly in English.
A detailed question should be answered with hunting for the required information.

### Participle examples used in engineering

The circuit designer actuates (or: turns) the potentiometer increasing the voltage to 12 V.
The operator pressed the button, putting the plant into operation.
The electrical erector pressed key b1, observing the indicating lights of the control panel.
Depressing push-button b11 causes relay d1 to operate, holding itself by contact d1-7/8.

## Unit 9.2

### Lifting the turbine casing cover*

Remove the sheet-metal lagging in the vicinity of the steam-pipe joint. Then break the pipe joint or remove a length of steam piping. Disconnect any pressure gauge connections and gland housings. Insert the guide pillars. Extreme caution must be exercised whilst lifting the cover, the guide pillars being closely watched to make sure nothing is fouling. When high enough, the cover may be run clear or it may be secured above the rotor on supporting columns. The columns must be flanged at each end, with bolt holes for fastening to the cover and lower casing.

35

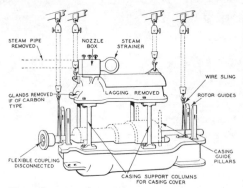

## Drawing captions

*casing cover* Gehäusedeckel
*casing guide pillars* Gehäuseführungsstäbe; pillar sonst auch: Pfeiler, Pfosten, Säule, Ständer
*casing support columns* Gehäuseauflageständer; support columns sonst auch: Stützpfeiler
*coupling* Kupplung
*glands, carbon type* Stopfbüchse, Kohleausführung (nicht mehr für Grossturbinen verwendet)
*lagging* Verkleidung
*nozzle box* Düsenkasten, Düsenkammer, Turbineneintrittsgehäuse

*rotor guides* Rotorführungsstangen
*steam-pipe* Dampfrohr
*steam strainer* Dampfreinigungssieb
*wire sling* Drahtschlinge

*to lift* abheben, aufnehmen - *turbine casing cover* Turbinengehäusedeckel - *to remove* entfernen, abbauen, abnehmen, abmontieren - *sheet-metal lagging* Blechverkleidung - *in the vicinity* in der Nähe, herum - *steam-pipe joint* Dampfrohranschluss; joint sonst auch: Stoss, Verbindung, Fuge, Schweissstoss - *to break* lösen; sonst auch: brechen, abreissen, ausschalten, unterbrechen - *length of pipe* Rohrlänge, Rohrstück - *to disconnect* lösen; sonst auch: trennen, abschalten, unterbrechen - *pressure gauge* (US: gage) Druckanzeiger - *connection* Anschluss - *gland housing* Stopfbüchsengehäuse - *to insert* einsetzen, einstecken - *guide pillar* Führungsstab, Führungsstange - *extreme* äusserst, höchst - *caution* Vorsicht, Behutsamkeit - *to exercise* ausüben, anwenden - *to watch closely* genau beobachten - *fouling* im Wege, unklar, eingeklemmt sein - *to run clear* frei sein - *to secure* sichern - *supporting column* Auflageständer - *to flange* anflanschen - *bolt hole* Bolzenloch - *fastening* Befestigung - *lower casing* Gehäuseunterteil

# Unit 9.3

## Melting is the secret of making joints*

The PERA-Production Engineering Research Association laboratory at Melton Mowbray has developed, and is now licensing out a plastics-joining process known as Peramelt. A sheet of perforated metal or metal gauze is placed between two plastic components which are then heated until they melt while pressure is applied. The metal acts as an anchor, allowing previously impracticable shapes to be fabricated from plastic.
The finished joint, which takes only five seconds to form, is normally stronger than the components being cemented. Two different materials can be attached; the joints are neat in appearance and suitable for making or repairing high-quality products. Window frames, decorative trims for cars and heavy-duty plastic tanks are among the applications envisaged.

*to melt* schmelzen - *secret* Geheimnis - *joint* Verbindung(sstelle) - *Production Engineering Research Association* etwa: Forschungsverband für Produktionstechnik - *laboratory* Laboratorium - *to develop* entwickeln - *to license out* konzessionieren, lizensieren - *process* Verfahren, Prozess - *sheet of metal* Metallplatte - *perforated* gelocht, perforiert - *gauze* Drahtgeflecht - *to place* legen - *component* Teil, Stück - *to heat* erwärmen, erhitzen - *while pressure is applied* unter Druckbelastung - *to act as* dienen als - *anchor* Anker - *to allow* ermöglichen, erlauben - *previous(ly)* ursprünglich, vorher - *impracticable* unhandlich, unausführbar - *shape* Form - *to be fabricated* hergestellt werden - *finished* fertig, fertiggestellt - *to cement* kitten (auf herkömmliche Art) - *to attach* zusammenfügen - *neat* sauber - *appearance* Aussehen, Erscheinen - *suitable* geeignet - *high-quality* von hoher Qualität - *window-frame* Fensterrahmen - *de-corative* dekorativ, Zier . . . - *trim* Ausstattung - *heavy-duty* hier: dauerhaft - *application* Anwendung, Einsatz - *to envisage* ins Auge fassen, beabsichtigen

## Unit 9.4

### Circuit diagram showing principle of automatic swivelling of deburring device for a milling machine*

On reaching the feed limit position, limit switch b31 is activated. Thereupon the feed reverses, allowing the limit switch to return to its normal position. The resulting voltage pulse energises time-lag relay d1. Contacts d1-3/4 close instantaneously, energising solenoid valve s1 which causes the deburring device (not shown) to swivel in. After a preset period elapses, contacts d1-3/4 open, solenoid valve d1 de-energises and the deburring device swivels out.

*circuit diagram* Stromlaufplan - *principle* Prinzip - *swivelling* Schwenken; to swivel sonst auch: drehen - *deburring device* Entgratungsvorrichtung; device sonst auch: Gerät - *milling maching* Fräsmaschine - *on reaching* beim Erreichen - *feed limit position* Ende (Endstellung) des Vorschubs - *limit switch* Endschalter - *to activate* betätigen - *to reverse* umkehren - *to allow* gestatten - *resulting* sich (hieraus) ergebend - *voltage pulse* Spannungs(im)puls - *to energise* erregen (Relais), betätigen, anreizen - *time-lag relay* Zeitrelais, (Zeit-) Verzögerungsrelais - *instantaneous(ly)* sofort, augenblicklich - *solenoid valve* Magnetventil - *to cause* veranlassen, bewirken; sonst auch: verursachen - *to swivel in* einschwenken - *preset* vorher eingestellt - *period* Zeit(raum) - *to elapse* verstreichen - *to de-energise* zum Abfall bringen, entregen - *to swivel out* zurückschwenken, ausschwenken

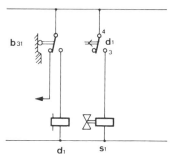

## Unit 9.5

### Selection procedure

I can never quite believe that people in search of a job are prepared to suffer the indignities heaped upon them by some sorts of selection procedure managements concoct. For instance, to check on a girl's marital status by resorting to a lie detector, as is alleged to be practised by some large American companies, seems to me base. But there are other ways. I heard recently of a computer company which insists that all its trainee executives are put through a programming course. The course book opens with several pages of exhortation on how success will depend on the trainee's ability to follow orders diligently, enthusiastically and, above all obediently. Then there follows an instruction to skip the next few pages and turn immediately to page so-and-so. Those whose curiosity is not under control find themselves reading a page on which is printed a stern warning that failure in the future to do as they are told will result in a much more serious reprimand. Yes, baas, I'se sorry, bwana, forgive, sahib . . .

*selection procedure* Auswahlverfahren - *in search of a job* bei der Stellungsuche - *prepared* bereit; sonst auch: vorbereiten - *to suffer* (er)dulden, erlauben; sonst auch: leiden - *indignity* unwürdige Behandlung, Demütigung, Kränkung - *to heap upon* auslassen (an); sonst auch: überschütten - *to concoct* aushecken, sich ausdenken - *to check on* nachprüfen, kontrollieren - *marital status* Familienstand - *to resort to* anwenden, Gebrauch machen - *lie detector* Lügendetektor - *to allege* behaupten; sonst auch: vorbringen - *to practise* praktizieren - *base* gemein, niederträchtig; sonst auch: minderwertig, unedel - *recently* kürzlich - *to insist* darauf bestehen - *trainee executive* in Ausbildung befindlicher leitender Angestellter - *to put someone through* jemanden unterziehen, durchlaufen lassen - *programming course* Programmierkurs - *exhortation* Ermahnung; sonst auch: Zureden- *success* Erfolg, Gelingen - *to depend on* abhängen von - *ability* Fähigkeit - *to follow orders* Anweisungen (Befehle) befolgen - *diligent(ly)* gewissenhaft; sonst auch: fleissig - *enthusiastical(ly)* begeistert - *above all* vor allem - *obedient(ly)* gehorsam, unterwürfig - *to skip* überschlagen, überspringen - *to turn to* sich ... zuwenden - *immediate(ly)* direkt, unverzüglich, sofort - *curiosity* Neugier - *to print* drucken - *stern* hart, streng - *failure* Versagen; sonst auch: Ausfall, Fehler - *to result in* zur Folge haben - *serious* schwerwiegend, ernst - *reprimand* Verweis, ernster Tadel

Georg Möllerke
**Im Ausland unterwegs**
Technicians and Engineers Abroad
1996. 98 S., 19 Abb.
18,5 x 12 cm. Br.
DM 20,00/öS 148,00/sFr 20,00
ISBN 3-18-401572-6

Der ins Ausland reisende Techniker kennt meist „seine" englischen Spezialausdrücke, aber gewisse Wendungen der fachlichen Umgangssprache fallen ihm einfach nicht ein. Da wird er froh sein, wenn er sich im Flugzeug noch rasch ein wenig in dem Taschenbuch umsehen und auf die bevorstehenden Gesprächssituationen vorbereiten kann. Kernstück dieses „technischen Sprachführers" sind neun Episoden „The experiences of Bob Keller, an engineer". Auf kurzweilige Art werden hier die Erlebnisse eines Ingenieurs auf seiner Kanadareise geschildert.

**GRATISFAX**
Inland 01 30/1 20-133
VDI-Mitglieder erhalten 10 % Preisnachlaß, auch im Buchhandel.

Postfach 10 10 54, 40001 Düsseldorf
Telefon 02 11/61 88-0, Telefax 02 11/61 88-133

# Lesson 10

## Unit 10.1

### The gerund

The gerund (Gerundium) has exactly the same form as the present participle (Präsenspartizip): working, operating, checking, controlling etc. It can be used in the following ways:

### 1. As a subject of a sentence
Designing a printed circuit board requires patience.
Die Konstruktion (das Konstruieren, Entwerfen) einer Leiterplatte (oder: einer gedruckten Schaltung) erfordert Geduld.

### 2. After prepositions
The engineer insisted on commissioning the system himself.
Der Ingenieur bestand darauf, die Anlage selbst in Betrieb zu setzen. (One cannot say: He insisted to start the system . . .)

### 3. After certain verbs
I am looking forward to seeing you again.
Ich freue mich (schon) darauf, Sie wieder zu sehen.

### 4. In noun compounds
Breaking capacity. Ausschaltvermögen (bei Leistungsschaltern).

### Some examples for using the gerund after prepositions

*That draughtswoman is good at designing (or: drawing) clearly arranged key plans.*
Die Zeichnerin (dort) kann (oder: ist in der Lage) übersichtliche Schlüsselpläne (zu) zeichnen.

*He is thinking of re-writing the last part of the specification.*
Er denkt (oder: erwägt) den letzten Teil der Spezifikation (oder: des Pflichtenheftes) neu zu schreiben (oder: zu überarbeiten).

*I'm sorry for keeping you waiting.*
Es tut mir leid, dass Sie warten mussten.

*The electronics engineer raised the money for starting his own business by selling his big car.*
Der Elektroniker beschaffte sich das Geld für den Aufbau des eigenen Geschäfts, indem er sein grosses Auto verkaufte.

The gerund must be used after the following verbs.
*admit* zugeben, zulassen, einlassen
*anticipate* erwarten, erhoffen, im voraus tun
*avoid* (ver)meiden, ausweichen
*consider* erwägen, nachdenken, ansehen als
*defer* nachgeben, aufschieben
*delay* verzögern, verschieben
*deny* abstreiten, leugnen
*detest* verabscheuen, hassen
*dread* (sehr) fürchten, (grosse) Angst haben
*enjoy* geniessen, Freude haben an
*excuse* entschuldigen, verzeihen
*fancy* sich vorstellen, meinen, halten für
*finish* (be)enden, abschliessen, vollenden
*forgive* vergeben, verzeihen
*imagine* sich vorstellen, anschaulich darstellen
*involve* angehen, betreffen, mit sich bringen, verknüpfen
*keep* (continue) dabeibleiben, festhalten, fortfahren
*mind* (object) einwenden, reklamieren
*miss* verpassen, vermissen, fehlschlagen
*pardon* verzeihen, entschuldigen
*postpone* verschieben
*prevent* verhindern, verhüten
*recollect* sich erinnern
*resent* übelnehmen, verübeln, sich ärgern über
*resist* widerstehen
*risk* riskieren, wagen
*save* (e.g. trouble) ersparen
*stop* (an)halten
*suggest* vorschlagen, hindeuten
*understand* verstehen
The gerund is used also after the expressions: can't stand (endure), can't help (prevent/avoid), it's no use / no good, and after the adjective worth.

## Gerund examples

*The agent denied having been in the test station.*
Der Agent stritt es ab, im Versuchslokal gewesen zu sein.

*Forgive my interrupting you (or: forgive me for interrupting you).*
Verzeih mir, dass ich dich unterbrochen habe.

*The engineer suggested waiting with the tests till dawn.*
Der Ingenieur schlug vor, mit dem Versuch bis zur Morgendämmerung zu warten.

*It's no use looking through the magnifying-glass.*
Es hat keinen Zweck (bzw.: es lohnt sich nicht), durch das Vergrösserungsglas zu sehen.

*I couldn't resist buying that oscilloscope.*
Ich konnte nicht widerstehen, das Oszilloskop zu kaufen.

*Putting in a new window will involve (or: mean) cutting away part of the roof.*

*Ein neues Fenster einsetzen bedeutet, einen Teil des Daches wegreissen.*

*I don't anticipate meeting any opposition.*
Ich erwarte keine Opposition (oder: keinen Widerstand).

*The erecting engineer postponed making a decision till he had been given more information.*
Der Montage-Ingenieur (oder: Monteur) schob die Entscheidung auf, bis ihm mehr Unterlagen (oder: Informationen) zur Verfügung standen.

*Fancy having to get up at five a.m. every day!*
Stell dir vor, jeden Tag um fünf Uhr morgens aufstehen!

*The training officer dreads getting old.*
Der Ausbildungsleiter fürchtet sich vor dem Altwerden.

### Exercises
Form gerund sentences using the following verbs: enjoy, finish, imagine, involve, save.

# Unit 10.2

## Faulty control equipment *

*First of all, we must remove the top cover.*
Als erstes müssen wir die obere Abdeckung (oder: den Deckel) entfernen (oder: abnehmen).

*Then we must remove the rear plate.*
Dann müssen wir die hintere Platte abnehmen.

*Now I'm going to draw out the printed-circuit board.*
Jetzt werde ich die Leiterplatte herausziehen.

*I'm disconnecting the feeder cable now.*
Nun werde ich das Speisekabel entfernen (oder: abklemmen, lösen).

*Both current transformers must also be removed.*
Beide Stromwandler müssen auch ausgebaut (oder: entfernt, herausgenommen) werden.

*The terminal block must be unscrewed.*
Der Klemmblock ist abzuschrauben.

*The second diode is defective.*
Die zweite Diode ist defekt.

*Hand me the small screw-driver, please.*
Reich mir bitte den kleinen Schraubenzieher.

*I'm now removing the diode.*
Ich nehme jetzt die Diode heraus.

*We needn't strip down the whole device.*
Wir brauchen nicht das ganze Gerät auseinanderzunehmen.

*Would you please check the diode.*
Würdest du bitte die Diode prüfen.

*Is there a spare diode?*
Ist da (noch) eine Reservediode?

*I'm afraid there's no spare diode.*
Ich fürchte, wir haben keine Reservediode (mehr).

*Don't worry, Metroniks stock this type of diode.*
Keine Bange, Metroniks hat diesen Diodentyp auf Lager.

*Before we continue the controller should be cleaned.*
Ehe wir weitermachen, sollte das Steuergerät (oder: der Kontroller) gereinigt werden.

# Unit 10.3

## Finnish company tackles a burning problem*

Two Finnish diesel district heating systems are breaking with accepted practice by using afterburners to increase efficiency thus avoiding the need for auxiliary boilers. Afterburners, which use air-rich exhaust to burn fuel, are widely used in gas turbines but have hitherto not been tried with diesel heating schemes.

One problem of combining heat and electricity production in district heating schemes is regulating the proportion of each form of energy produced. A steam turbine generating set produces up to four times more heat than electricity, whereas for a diesel-driven plant the proportions are about equal. This has led to increased adoption of diesel «total energy» units for district heating in Scandinavia.

Sometimes where diesels are used there is a demand for more heat which is usually met by the installation of auxiliary boilers. But burning more fuel in the exhaust may cost less.

The Kiuruvesi plant in northern Finland, which has just become operational, puts this idea into practice. It provides 2 MW of electricity and up to 6 MW of heat in the form of hot water for district heating. A second plant, Marianhamina in southern Finland, is due to start up next year with an electrical capacity of 8 MW and up to 24 MW of heat.

The innovation should mean that the overall efficiency of the plant increases from 81 to 89 per cent. No auxiliary boiler is required, but the afterburner needs a number of regulatory circuits because the burner has to operate with widely varying gas flows as engine power is altered. This could make such plants more expensive than the «conventional» solution of a package boiler and an exhaust gas boiler.

*to tackle* anpacken, in Angriff nehmen - *diesel district heating system* Diesel-Fernheizungsanlage - *to break with* hier: abweichen von, aufhören mit - *accepted* allgemein (anerkannt) - *afterburner* Nachbrenner - *to increase* erhöhen - *efficiency* Wirkungsgrad - *to avoid* vermeiden - *auxiliary* Hilfs . . ., Zusatz . . . - *exhaust* Abgas - *fuel* Brenn-, Treibstoff - *hitherto* bis jetzt, bisher - *scheme* System, Anlage - *to combine* kombinieren, verbinden - *electricity production* Elektrizitätserzeugung - *proportion* Anteil, Verhältnis - *steam* Dampf - *to generate* erzeugen - *driven* (an)getrieben - *plant* Anlage - *equal* gleich, entsprechend - *led* (to lead) geführt - *adoption* Übernahme, Anwendung - *unit* Anlage - *demand* Bedarf, Nachfrage - *met by* (to meet) hier: gedeckt durch - *operational* betriebsbereit, einsatzfähig - *idea* Idee, Gedanke - *to provide* liefern - *is due to start* wird den Betrieb aufnehmen, beginnen - *electrical capacity* elektrische Leistung - *innovation* Neuerung - *to mean* bedeuten - *overall* Gesamt . . . - *to require* benötigen - *number* Anzahl - *regulatory circuit* Regulierkreislauf - *to operate* arbeiten, funktionieren - *wide(ly) varying* weit variierend - *gas flow* Gasstrom - *engine power* Motorenleistung - *to alter* ändern - *expensive* teuer - *conventional* herkömmlich, üblich - *solution* Lösung - *package boiler* Kompakt-Heizkesselanlage

# Unit 10.4

## How to do a good job

Volvo, the Swedish car makers, have opened an assembly plant at Kalmar in the south of the country which shows that all mills don't have to be dark and satanic. The absenteeism rate, that infallible indicator of people's feelings about the work they are doing, is almost a third of what it is at the other Volvo plants. Instead of the tyranny of the assembly line the work is done on battery-driven platforms directed to any part of the plant by control wires embedded in the floor, so that the teams of men, each numbering between 15 and 25 can work at a pace that suits them. Each team has its own rest room complete with fridge, cooker and coffee machine. The place is so quiet men can talk to one another without having to shout. There is plenty of light and air. The managing director estimates that production costs will be the same as in the old-fashioned sort of plant – or even less. Is all this possible, as Agnelli the Fiat king believes, only in the social climate of Sweden with its high levels of general education? If true, it's shaming for the rest of us industrial brutes.

car maker Autohersteller - *assembly plant* Montagewerk - *mill* Fabrik; sonst auch: Mühle - *satanic* teuflisch, satanisch - *absenteeism rate* Abwesenheitsrate - *infallible* unfehlbar - *indicator* Anzeiger - *instead of* an Stelle von - *tyranny* Tyrannei - *assembly line* Fliessband - *to direct* leiten - *control wires* Steuerleitungen - *to embed* einlassen, einbetten - *floor* (Fuss-)Boden - *pace* Tempo; sonst auch: Gangart - *to suit* passen - *rest room* Ruheraum - *fridge* (refrigerator) Kühlschrank - *cooker* Kocher - *to shout* schreien, brüllen - *to estimate* schätzen - *to believe* glauben - *climate* Klima - *level* Niveau - *general education* Allgemeinbildung - *shaming* beschämend - *industrial brutes* unvernünftige Industriemenschen

# Unit 10.5

## Putting a tiger in your boiler*

The latest firm to start exploiting the fact that energy costs can be cut dramatically by applying low technology, «good housekeeping» principles is the Esso oil company. The firm last week launched a marketing operation aimed at selling to the industrial world an audio-visual training kit which teaches people how to operate boilers properly. This might seem a simple technique but is apparently one to which many industries pay little attention, at an estimated cost of £ 60 million yearly in wasted fuel.
Esso started looking at the problem in its own plant about five years ago and came up with the scheme for training its own operators. The move was initiated by recognising that «automatic» boiler controls were not all they promised to be and that training the people who were operating them was important. Esso found it could save £ 2000 a year on the running of each of the 21 boilers at the company's distribution and storage plants: if only half the saving was reproduced for all the 60 000 similar industrial boilers in the UK the net gain would be £ 60 million or roughly five per cent of total running costs.
The firm hopes to sell up to 100 of the kits, each of which costs £ 45 and consists of two hours of slides and tape that can be used in a day's full training session. The scheme was developed with the aid of the audio-visual unit at Leicester University's engineering department.

*to exploit* ausnutzen (kommerziell) - *fact* Tatsache - *energy costs* Energiekosten - *to apply* anwenden - *technology* Technologie - *«housekeeping»* «Haushalten» - *principle* Prinzip - *to launch* lancieren, beginnen; sonst auch: (Schiff) vom Stapel lassen - *marketing operation* Verkaufs(werbe)aktion - *aimed at* mit dem Ziel - *industrial* Industrie . . . - *audio-visual* audiovisuell - *training kit* Ausbildungs-, Schulungsausrüstung - *to operate* bedienen, arbeiten mit - *proper(ly)* richtig, genau - *technique* Verfahren, Technik - *apparent(ly)* anscheinend - *to pay attention to* Beachtung schenken - *estimated* geschätzt - *wasted* verschwendet, vergeudet - *fuel* Brenn-, Treibstoff - *plant* Anlage, Werk - *to come up* herausbringen, produzieren - *scheme* Plan, Projekt - *to train* ausbilden - *operators* Bedienungspersonal - *move* Massnahme - *to initiate* einleiten, auslösen - *to recognise* erkennen - *control* Kontrolle, Steuerung - *to promise* versprechen - *important* wichtig - *to save* einsparen; sonst auch: retten - *distribution* Verteil . . ., Vertrieb . . . - *storage* Lager . . ., Depot . . . - *to reproduce* wiederholen, reproduzieren - *net gain* Nettogewinn - *rough(ly)* ungefähr, annähernd - *running costs* Betriebskosten - *to consist of* bestehen aus, sich zusammensetzen aus - *slide* Dia(positiv) - *tape* (Ton)Band - *to develop* entwickeln - *aid* Hilfe, Unterstützung - *unit* Anlage - *engineering department* technische Abteilung

# The experiences of an engineer

This is a series depicting events in the working life of Ronald Newman, head of a section of Berdy & Myles, a large engineering firm based in Sherborne.

## Episode 1

### An erecting engineer relates his experiences abroad

David Freeman, just back from Argentina, talks about some problems encountered in putting a large diesel engine into operation.

Anne:
Did you see the note on your desk?
Ronald:
No – what note? Oh yes, here it is. David's coming in to see us at 10 o'clock.
Anne:
Yes, he wants to report on his trip to Argentina. On the phone he said he had an interesting story for us.
Ronald:
Whenever David goes abroad he always comes back with some thrilling story or other.
Anne:
You're telling me! I'll never forget that cliffhanger about his emergency landing in the African jungle. Nobody can tell us there isn't any adventure these days.
Ronald:
No, indeed. Not when you think of David.
(A knock at the door)
David:
Good morning, Anne. Good morning, Ron.
Ronald: 'Morning!
Anne:
Hello, David.
David:
I'm a bit earlier than expected. I hope you don't mind.
Ronald:
Not at all. Thanks for the telex – it was good to hear you'd got the diesel engine running properly. And nice to have you back so soon. I'm glad it only took four days.
David:
Well, the actual work only took me five hours.
Anne:
Tell us all about it.
David:
Well, it's an odd story. The manager of the power plant told me the diesel engine had been installed according to factory instructions, but it wouldn't start. When I suggested trying to start it up, he said, «If you can get that engine going, we'll give you four weeks holiday in Argentina – all expenses paid!»
Anne:
Quite a challenge!
Ronald:
Yes – though I'm sure there isn't any diesel engine you can't put into operation. Well – go on.
David:
I barred the engine by hand and checked that valve and pump action were both in order. After that, I knew the problem must be something simple. But what?
Ronald:
Perhaps the fuel supply?
David:
No, everything seemed to be in order. Then I cranked the engine with the air starting valve. She began to roll, but stopped after a few turns. Then I asked the manager for a long extension ladder to reach the roof.
He couldn't see why, in fact he said, «What we really need is a stick of dynamite to get this going». Well, I put the ladder up against the exhaust pipe, which extended through the roof. And then I climbed up to the 10 inch connecting flange just under the roof where the muffler was mounted.
Anne:
I suppose you already knew what was wrong?
David:

43

Well, I had an idea. When the engine had first started firing, I'd noticed a small whiff of smoke escaping from the flanged joint. So I asked the mechanic to remove the steel blanking flange from between the pipe flanges. It hadn't been removed when the unit was installed.
Anne:
And did the engine start then?
David:
Yes, this time it started without any trouble.
Ronald:
Congratulations! And how about the holiday in Argentina?
David: Oh – next year, probably.
(Ronald and Anne laugh)
Anne:
Some people have all the luck.

*experiences* Erfahrungen, Erlebnisse - *to depict* schildern, darstellen, beschreiben - *event* Begebenheit, Vorfall - *erecting engineer* Montage-Ingenieur, Monteur - *to relate* berichten, erzählen (über, von) - *abroad* im Ausland - *to encounter* stossen auf, begegnen - *cliffhanger* spannende Geschichte; wörtlich: über jemanden, der an einer Klippe hängt - *emergency landing* Notlandung - *adventure* Abenteuer - *properly* ordnungsgemäss - *odd* seltsam, komisch - *expenses* Ausgaben, Kosten - *challenge* Herausforderung - *to bar* (durch)drehen - *valve* Ventil - *fuel supply* Brennstoffversorgung - *to crank* (durch)drehen - *extension ladder* Ausziehleiter - *roof* Dach - *stick of dynamite* Stück (oder: Paket) Dynamit - *exhaust pipe* Auspuffrohr - *to climb up* hinaufsteigen - *connecting flange* Anschlussflansch - *muffler* Geräuschdämpfer - *to mount* anordnen, montieren - *to fire* zünden - *whiff of smoke* kleine Rauchwolke - *to escape* hervorkommen, entkommen - *flanged joint* Flanschverbindung - *to remove* entfernen - *steel blanking flange* Blindflansch aus Stahl (Scheibe zum Absperren einer Rohrleitung)

# Episode 2

## Preliminary work on obtaining a major order

Ronald Newman and Clark Kimball, an engineer in Ronald's section, discuss the chances of obtaining a large order worth about half a million pounds. It involves the delivery and installation of two 800 kW diesel-generator sets. The customer is the Toronto Municipal Council, the consulting engineers – Winter and Wilmore of Manchester.
(A knock at the door)
Anne:
Come in.
Clark:
Good morning, Anne.
Anne:
Good morning, Clark. Do sit down.
Clark:
Thanks.
Anne:
Ron's in Bertram's office, but he'll be back in a second.
Clark:
What's going on? Ronald sounded so mysterious on the phone.
Anne:
He wants to put every possible effort into obtaining that Canadian diesel engine contract. Two of our manufacturing sections are short of work at present, as you know. And we've a great chance of obtaining the order.
Clark:
You mean, because we can meet the specifications on all points?
Anne:
That's right. And I think the F.S.T. device – the fail-safe starting system – is a good point in our favour.
(Ronald enters)
Ronald:
Ah – good to have you here, Clark. Now we can discuss the Canadian tender. (To Anne) Can I have a copy of Amendment D to the M.C. Toronto specifications?
Anne:
It's on your desk.
Ronald:
Ah yes, thank you, Clark, this is just the order we so urgently need. Here, have a look. They want a quotation for two 800 kW diesel-

Clark:
generator sets, not 600 kW as previously stated.
Clark:
Well, that means new calculations throughout – and new diagrams.
Ronald:
I know it's a bit of a nuisance, but it'll be well worth it if we're awarded the contract. Repeat orders would follow in two years' time. Now, the contract's being supervised by Winter and Wilmore, who worked out the specifications. Luckily, I know Mr. Elliott, the engineer in charge of their entire mechanical section. He'll be responsible for evaluating the bids and he'll be making the final recommendations to the Toronto Municipal Council with regard to the successful tender.
Clark:
Then he's certainly the most important man. Winter and Wilmore are based in Manchester, aren't they?
Ronald:
Yes, that's where they have their head office. I think you should go up there as soon as possible to see Mr. Elliott and discuss details of the specifications with him.
Clark:
As far as I can see, the specifications are so clearly written, there's nothing left open to question.
Ronald:
Oh, I'm sure they are – Mr. Elliott's an excellent engineer. But, you see, there's something else I'm after.
Clark:
What do you mean?
Ronald:
Well, Clark, if we really want to get this order, we can't just hand in our tender and sit back. We'd be very lucky if we got the order that way, without any special effort. There'll be about six competitors after this contract, you know, and it's every man for himself. Now, didn't you tell me we could offer a more efficient water cooling system than was stipulated in the specifications – and at no extra cost?

Clark:
That's right.
Ronald:
Then I suggest you discuss this important point with Mr. Elliott.
Clark:
Hmm – good idea.
Ronald:
You must try and convince him that we're the most helpful and cooperative company he's ever had dealings with. It's most important to bring out the necessity for all the items shown in your preliminary plans, so that he'll understand our tender drawings and calculations at the evaluation stage.
Clark:
Yes – I see your point. With this sort of approach, we'll have a much better chance of winning the order.

*preliminary work* Vorarbeit - *to obtain* erhalten, gelangen zu - *major order* grosser Auftrag - *section* Gruppe - *to involve* betreffen, einschliessen; sonst auch: verwickeln - *customer* Kunde - *Municipal Council* etwa: Stadtrat - *to sound* sich anhören, klingen, tönen - *mysterious* geheimnisvoll - *effort* Anstrengung, Aufwand - *to meet* hier: erfüllen - *device* Gerät - *fail-safe starting system* Sicherheitsanlaufsystem - *in our favour* zu unseren Gunsten - *tender* Angebot - *amendment* Zusatz - *quotation* Preisangebot - *nuisance* Plage, Unangenehmes, Unfug - *to award* zuerkennen - *repeat order* Folgeauftrag - *to supervise* überwachen - *engineer in charge* leitender Ingenieur, zuständiger Fachmann - *to evaluate* auswerten - *recommendation* Empfehlung - *with regard to* hinsichtlich des - *competitor* Konkurrent - *efficient* leistungsfähig - *to stipulate* festlegen, (Vereinbarung) treffen - *to convince* überzeugen - *cooperative* hilfsbereit - *dealings* Geschäfte - *necessity* Notwendigkeit, Bedeutung - *item* Punkt, Posten - *drawing* Zeichnung - *evaluation stage* Stadium der Auswertung - *approach* Methode, Verfahren; sonst auch: Annäherung

# Episode 3

## Meeting an important customer

Mr. Paul Hansen, Manager of the Engineering Department of Carroll Chemicals in Sudbury, Canada, is visiting Berdy & Myles. He meets Ronald to discuss the purchase of six diesel engines, each rated at 4,800 h.p. and equipped with the «Berdy Diagnostic System».

(A knock at the door)
Mr. Hansen:
Good morning. My name's Hansen.
Anne:
Good morning. Ah yes – you're Mr. Hansen of Carroll Chemicals, aren't you? We've been expecting you. I'll take you in to see Mr. Newman right away.
(Anne enters Ron's office)
Ron – Mr. Hansen's here.
Ronald:
Ah, good morning, Mr. Hansen. How do you do.
Mr. Hansen:
How do you do.
Ronald:
Sit down, won't you? Plane was a bit late, was it?
Mr. Hansen:
Yes – nearly an hour late. There were quite a few planes in the air waiting to land before us.
Ronald: You've been here before, haven't you?
Mr. Hansen:
Several times. Last time I came I met Mr. Mallowan. By the way, I'd like to see him too.
Ronald:
Mr. Mallowan retired more than a year ago. I'm his successor.
Mr. Hansen:
Oh, I see. I hadn't realised Mr. Mallowan was near retirement age. Look – if you agree, Mr. Newman, I'd like to have a talk with him all the same. This evening, perhaps?
Ronald:
Yes, of course. I'll try and arranged it.
Mr. Hansen:
Well now, let's get down to business. We're very much interested in your large diesel engines, fully equipped with the «Berdy Diagnostic System» as supplied for marine diesel engines. You've already had a considerable amount of experience with this system, haven't you?
Ronald:
Yes indeed. We've been equipping our large engines with this diagnostic system for the last three years. And it's proved most reliable. It really is a great asset to be able to check the cylinder and piston wear at any time, simply by pressing a button on the data logger.
Mr. Hansen:
So that it's no longer necessary to dismantle an engine in order to inspect the condition of pistons and cylinders?
Ronald:
Exactly. Thanks to electronics. Look, before going into detail, would you like a cup of coffee – or something to eat?
Mr. Hansen:
I could do with some coffee.
Ronald:
Good. Let's go and get some, shall we?

*customer* Kunde - *purchase* Kauf - *rated at* mit einer (Nenn-)Leistung von - *to equip* ausrüsten *diagnostic system* Diagnosesystem - *to retire* in den Ruhestand treten, sich zurückziehen - *successor* Nachfolger - *to realise* realisieren, (klar) erkennen - *retirement age* Pensionsalter - *to supply* liefern - *marine diesel engine* Schiffsdieselmotor - *a considerable amount* eine ganze Menge - *to prove* sich erweisen - *reliable* betriebssicher, zuverlässig - *asset* Vorteil - *piston wear* Kolbenverschleiss, -abnutzung - *necessary* notwendig - *to dismantle* auseinandernehmen

# Episode 4

## Introducing a test engineer

Paul Murray, a mechanical engineer appointed to a special Diesel Engine Test Group, has just arrived. As Ronald is due to attend a further meeting with Mr. Hansen, he asks his assistant, Anne Adams, to introduce Paul Murray to their colleagues.

Ronald:
Anne, could you perhaps help me by introducing our new colleague, Paul Murray, to the staff – starting with the senior engineers? As you know, I'm rather busy just now preparing for that meeting with Mr. Hansen.
Anne:
Yes, of course. We're lucky to have found such a good man.
Ronald:
I think so too. He'll be working in E.T.4 Group, Test Station 1.
Anne:
I can't understand why a company like Watson and Reed Engines didn't appreciate his talents more.
Ronald:
Oh, they did. However, Barry Turner – whom I met during my visit to Stanford University – was his former head of department. Need I say more?
Anne:
Ah, I remember, you told me – an unpleasant man to work for. Someone like Barry Turner would never have a chance in our company.
Ronald:
No – although he applied for a post here, you know. But he was turned down, thanks to Mr. Baker, our Managing Director. Well, we mustn't keep Mr. Murray waiting any longer, Anne. Would you call him in, please?
Anne:
Yes, of course.
(Goes to door and opens it)
Will you come in now, please, Mr. Murray?
Paul: Thank you.
Anne:
This is Mr. Newman, the head of our section.
Paul:
How do you do.
Ronald:
Good to have you with us, Mr. Murray. Look, I've asked Anne to take care of you for the time being. I'm afraid I have to attend a meeting. I look forward to seeing you later.
(Ronald leaves)
Anne:
I suppose you know that you've been appointed assistant to Mr. Milton, the head of E.T.4 Group. He's due to retire next winter. I'm sure you'll get on with him very well.
Paul:
That's good to hear. How's business?
Anne:
Not too bad. Some of our groups are working overtime. Two of the manufacturing sections aren't fully occupied – but they soon will be. Well, shall we make a start? I think we should go along to E.T.4 first, your group.

*to introduce* einführen, vorstellen - *to appoint* einsetzen, zuweisen, bestimmen - *to attend* beiwohnen - *staff* Angestellte; sonst auch: Stab - *senior engineer* älterer (oder: leitender) Ingenieur - *to appreciate* wertschätzen, anerkennen - *to apply for* sich bewerben um - *to turn down* ablehnen, abweisen - *I look forward* Ich freue mich (schon) darauf - *to retire* in den Ruhestand treten - *occupied* hier: ausgelastet; sonst: besetzt

# Episode 5

## Emergency call from Alaska

The engineers at Dingwall Power Station are in trouble. Due to extremely cold weather, with temperatures of minus forty-eight degrees Centigrade, their compressed-air plant is losing air. They urgently need replacement gaskets.

(Telephone ringing)
Anne:
Good morning, Berdy and Myles, Sherborne. Pardon, I didn't catch your name. (Pause) Ah yes, I can understand you now. You're Mr. Carlsson from Dingwall Power Station in Alaska. – No, Mr. Newman isn't in his office. He's expected back by about two o'clock. (Pause) You can tell me, I'll take it down. Go ahead, please. – The compressed-air plant for the 275 kV air-blast breakers in the outdoor switchyard is losing a considerable amount of air. – Leaks have been observed at most gasketed flange connections. We urgently need new gaskets. Those in use are of the 45G design, manufactured by Burns Brothers. Please provide the best design available. – We are reading minus forty-eight degrees Centigrade. – That's all? I'll get Mr. Newman to ring you back later today. Goodbye.
(Later)
Ronald:
Good afternoon, Anne.
Anne:
Oh hello, Ron. There's a message for you here.
Ronald: Thanks. Hmm – seems a pretty urgent affair. But there's no question of complete failure of the compressed-air plant?
Anne:
Oh no.
Ronald:
Well, I'll find out exactly what's going on. It's not really a job for our section, but I know Henry Carlsson well. Can you get me a line to Dingwall now?
Anne:
Ah yes, I'll get on to it, straight away.
(Some time later)
Brian:
Good afternoon, Ron.
Ronald:
Ah – thanks for getting here so quickly, Brian. Take a seat, won't you? Look, I'm really sorry to land you with an overseas trip at such short notice – especially on a Friday – but can you fly to Alaska tomorrow?
Brian:
Well, yes, I can. In fact, it'll suit me fine. I haven't been abroad for some time.
Ronald:
Good – then that's settled.
Brian:
What exactly is going in at Dingwall? I've a rough idea about it from Anne.
Ronald:
It's that gasket trouble again. You remember what happened three years ago – when we had to replace all the gaskets for the A2 system? Well, this time it seems to be even more serious.
Brian:
I thought we'd used the best gaskets available.
Ronald:
Yes, I thought so too. But in the meantime I've found out that it's White and Fox that really lead the field in this type of equipment.
Brian:
With regard to low temperatures as well?
Ronald:
Especially with regard to low temperatures. Their heavy-duty designs are guaranteed to withstand temperatures as low as minus sixty degrees Centigrade.
Brian:
Well, that's exactly what we need.
Ronald:
I've contacted a Mr. Manning at White and Fox. He's willing to meet you this evening.
Brian:
That's good, because we can't afford to lose any time. I'll arranged it immediately. That's all then, is it?
Ronald:
I think so. Good luck, Brian.
Brian:
Thanks. Goodbye, Ron.

*emergency call* (telefonischer) Notruf - *compressed-air plant* Druckluftanlage - *urgent(ly)* dringend - *replacement gaskets* Ersatzdichtungen - *to take it down* es aufschreiben, niederschreiben - *air-blast breaker* Druckluftschalter - *outdoor switchyard* Freiluftschaltanlage - *leak* Leck - *to observe* beobachten - *gasketed flange*

48

*connection* mit Dichtungen versehene Flanschverbindungen - *design* Konstruktion, Entwurf - *to provide* vorsehen, liefern - *available* erhältlich, verfügbar - *to read* hier ablesen - *message* Nachricht, Mitteilung - *failure* Ausfall, Versagen - *at short notice* kurzfristig - *to suit* passen - *settled* abgemacht - *rough* grob, ungenau -

*serious* ernst(haft) - *equipment* Ausrüstung, Gerät(e), Anlage(n) - *with regard to* hinsichtlich - *heavy-duty design* Ausführung für schwierige Betriebsbedingungen - *to contact* Verbindung aufnehmen - *to afford* es sich leisten - *immediate(ly)* umgehend, sofort

Artist's impression of creepy crawlies employed at the research laboratory, Ministry of Progress, Pulham Down.

# Focus on major engineering achievements

## Cruise Vessel "Oriana" at 25 knots

"Oriana" is the fastest cruise vessel now in service, sailing under the Red Ensign of P&O Cruises, London.
She was delivered by the Meyer Werft of Papenburg in Germany and combines most advanced technology with the comfort and style of traditional ocean liners.
The length is 260 m and breadth 32 m. "Oriana" is propelled by four non-reversible, four-stroke engines, with an output of 2 x 11,925 kW and 2 x 7,950 kW at 428 rpm. Each pair of engines transmits their power via a gearbox to a propeller shaft. Engine maker is MAN.
Four auxiliary diesel generator sets (MAN make), each rated at 4,420 kW, 514 rpm, provide the main electric power for this ship. Further there are two shaft generators and an emergency generator set.
Special mention should be made to the new emergency lighting system.
Experience gained from fires on board ships indicates that the normal emergency lighting, which is arranged at headheight, can be obscured by rising smoke. The low location lighting enables passengers to readily identify the escape routes and thus guarantees a safe evacuation.
The emergency plant is the first fitted low location lighting in the world. It consists of aluminium profiles incorporating LED (light-emitting diode) modules and the power supply units with rear-positioned batteries.
(The Motor Ship, London)

**cruise vessel** (cruise liner) Kreuzfahrtschiff - **knots** Knoten, 1,852 km/h (seamiles per hour) - **red ensign** rotes Zeichen (vor allem am Schornstein) - **to deliver** übergeben, abliefern - **advanced** hochentwickelt, fortgeschritten - **to propel** (an)treiben - **non-versible** nicht umsteuerbar - **four-stroke (diesel) engine** - Viertakt(diesel)motor - **output** (abgebene) Leistung - **rpm** (rev/min) revolutions per minute (U/min) - **to transmit** übertragen - **gearbox** Getriebe(kasten) - **shaft** Welle - **auxiliary** Hilfs... - **each rated at** jeder mit einer Nennleistung von - **to provide** liefern,

vorsehen - **main electric power** elektrisches Hauptnetz, Bord(haupt)netz - **emergency** Not... - **set** Aggregat, Satz - **experience** Erfahrung - **to gain** gewinnen - **to indicate** aufweisen, (auf)zeigen - **at headheight** in Kopfhöhe - **to obscure** sich verdunkeln, verfinstern - **to enable** ermöglichen, befähigen - **escape routes** Fluchtwege, Notausgänge - **rear-positoned** dahinter angebracht, auf der Rückseite befindlich

## End of the line

Take the largest, thinnest sheet of paper you can find. Fold it in half. Fold it in half again. After seven or eight folds, you will be unable to fold it by hand, as the sheet will have become as thick as a book. If 20 folds were possible, the stack of paper would dwarf your house.
At 40 folds, it would be well on its way to the moon. Seventy folds would take it to the nearest star and on as far again, light would take eight years to go from top to bottom, and after 100 folds, it would be more than ten billion light years across and span the whole universe.
This is the essence of exponential growth: very small amounts rapidly become astronomically large through simply doubling.
So large in fact that exponential growth is relegated to the realm of mathematics, nothing in the real world can keep it up for long. For the past 30 years, though, chips have improved in a thoroughly exponential way.
Just as Gordon Moore, one of the founders of Intel, predicted, chips have been steadily doubling in power every two years. Engineers have, in effect, folded the paper 15 times, each time doubling the number of components they could pack on to a chip. Transistors on chips are now less than 0.5 millionths of a metre across.
(Excerpt from The Economist, London)

**end of the line** Ende der Möglichkeiten, Ende der Leitung - **to fold** falten, umbiegen - **fold** Faltung - **unable** nicht in der Lage, unfähig - **stack** Stapel, Schichtung - **to dwarf** klein erscheinen lassen, in den Schatten stellen - **top to bottom** oben bis unten - **to span** umfassen, umspannen - **growth** Wachstum - **to relegate**

zuschreiben; sonst auch: verbannen - **realm** Bereich, Fachgebiet; sonst auch: Königreich - **chip** elektronischer Baustein, Plättchen - **founder** Gründer - **to predict** voraussagen - **component** Bauteil, Einzelteil - **to pack** einbauen, einpacken - **across** im Durchmesser

**Staying ahead of the competition: Heidelberger Druckmaschinen AG**

Johann Gutenberg, inventor of movable-type printing, would be proud of Heidelberger Druckmaschinen AG, Germany's best-known printing-press manufacturer.
Back in 1969, when a dollar could still buy four deutsche marks, the company racked up sales worth $96 million in 100 countries. In those days Heiderberger's average labor-and-benefit costs were the equivalent of just $2.50 an hour. This year the dollar dropped to only DM 1.40, and wage costs have rocketed to $40 an hour. Because exports are most often sold for dollars, such a run-up in costs might be expected to price Heidelberger right out of the market. But net sales have surged 863% since 1969, to an expected $2.5 billion this year, with three-quarters of the proceeds coming from exports to 180 countries. How the company managed to pull off this trick tells a lot about the ability of German industry to stay competitive.
Begun as a family-run foundry casting church bells in 1850, Heidelberger had started producing printing presses by 1860. From its headquarters in picturesque Heidelberg, the firm went international early on.
In 1926 it sold in Japan for the first time. In 1930, even as the U.S. was caught in the Great Depression, Heidelberger opened a sales office in New York. A year later came the debut of a company newsletter, the 'Heidelberg News', which is now read in 13 languages by printers around the world. Today Heidelberger operates the world's biggest printing-press center and dominates the international market, including the U.S., where it sells 27% of its output.
The key to Heidelberger's growth lies in the same business philosophy recently cited by the consulting firm McKinsey & Co., Inc., as central to the success of German firms: KISS (Keep It Simple, Stupid).
Heidelberger has steadfastly resisted horizontal integration into ancillary products such as printer's ink or paper, but has integrated vertically so totally that it produces virtually every part, mechanical or electronic, in its presses.
Manager Ulrich Mauser: "We could never have done this with an American-style banker always looking over our shoulders for the quarterly results."
The payoff came at May's international DRUPA printing fair in Düsseldorf, where Heidelberger was able to unveil a product line that was 85% new. "We sold $700 million worth right at the fair but it would be dangerous to dismiss the potential of Japanese competitors," Ulrich Mauser told TIME.
With an eye on the future, the company is also developing a global lead in the so-called direct-imaging printing. This is an infrared laser-driven procedure bypassing many of the steps in traditional offset printing.
(Excerpt from TIME, New York)

**to stay ahead** an der Spitze sein, vorn bleiben - **competition** Konkurrenz, Wettbewerb - **Johann Gutenberg** (1399-1468) aus Mainz, Erfinder des Buchdrucks, verwendete als erster bewegliche Lettern; Gutenberg-Museum, seit 1900 in Mainz - **inventor** Erfinder - **movable-type printing** Drucken mit bewegl. Lettern - **printing-press manufacturer** Druckmaschinen-Hersteller - **to rack up sales** Erfolg im Verkauf haben; to rack up auch: hochschrauben, hochgehen, in ein Gestell legen - **average** Durchschnitts... - **labo(u)r-and-benefit costs** Lohn- und Sozialkosten; sonst: Vorteil, Gewinn, Nutzen - **to drop** fallen - **wage costs** Lohnkosten - **to rocket** hochgehen, emporschnellen - **to price out of the market** aus dem Markt drücken (wegen der hohen Kosten) - **to surge** plötzlich steigen, hochgehen - **proceeds** Erlös, Ertrag, Gewinn - **to pull off** es schaffen, auch: (den Sieg) davontragen - **competitive** konkurrenzfähig - **foundry** Giesserei - **to cast** giessen; sonst auch: werfen - **headquarters** Stammhaus, "Hauptquartier" - **debut** Debüt, Antritt, Anfang - **to cite** zitieren, (als Beispiel) anführen - **ancillary** Neben... - **virtual(ly)** praktisch, wirklich - **to unveil** enthüllen - **to dismiss** hier: vernachlässigen; sonst: entlassen, abtreten - **competitor** Konkurrent - **to develop** entwickeln - **direct-imaging printing** Direktdrucksystem - **infrared** Infrarot... - **to bypass** auslassen, übergehen

### Such is accuracy

Precision engineering can now measure a shift in position of 0.0002 nanometres, or smooth a piece of quartz so that the rough peaks on its surface are no more than eight atoms tall. Such accuracy is bringing the mechanical engineer into a "realm where physics blends with chemistry", says Norman Brown of the Norman Brown of the Lawrence Livermore National Laboratory in the US.

Brown was speaking at a seminar on precision engineering, also known as "nanotechnology", at the Cranfield Institute of Technology last month. A nanometre is one-millionth of a millimetre; an atom is about 0.1 nanometres across. Nanotechnology's basic tools are diamond cutting edges that chip away pieces of material one micrometre across. Its products include optical parts for lasers, nozzles for ink-jet printers and components for computer memories.
(Excerpt from The Economist, London)

**accuracy** Genauigkeit, Präzision - **precision engineering** Präzisionstechnik - **to measure** messen - **shift** Verlagerung, Verschiebung - **to smooth** glätten - **piece of quartz** Quarzstück - **rough** grob, rauh - **peak** Spitze - **surface** Oberfläche - **realm** (sprich: relm) Bereich, Fachgebiet; sonst auch: Königreich - **to blend** sich verschmelzen, vermischen - **across** im Durchmesser - **cutting edge** Schneidkante - **to chip away** abspanen, wegschneiden - **nozzle** Düse - **ink-jet printer** Tintenstrahldrucker - **component** Bauteil, Einzelteil

### Keep an eye on the voltage level

If you use an accurate digital meter and check the mains voltage, you may well find it too high. Few people realise that even a small excess voltage can cut the life of a conventional tungsten lamp below the ususal 1000 hours, which are guaranteed.

There used to be a simple solution: Just buy bulbs rated for a higher voltage. But now that the whole of Britain's mains system is rated at 240 voltas, the chances of finding a 250 volt bulb are slim.

The key factor is that the 240 volt rating is only the average. The electricity boards are free to let the mains wander up or down by six per cent. That is a swing of 29 volts; more than the 14 volts above or below the 240 volt mean. Some homes will run above the 240 volt line and others below it. It depends on the length of underground cables between the home and the nearest transformer sub-station. The longer the cable run, the higher its resistance and the lower the voltage. To give distant homes adequate voltage, the sub-station has to push out a voltage which is above the mean. So homes close to the sub-station are likely to be well over the 240 volt level.

The electricity boards have also to cope with fluctuations of load, caused by weather changes, and peak or slack periods of demand.
(Excerpt from New Scientist, London)

**to keep an eye** beachten, Augenmerk richten auf - **voltage level** Spannungsniveau, -pegel - **mains voltage** Netzspannung - **tungsten lamp** Glühlampe; tungsten sonst: Wolfram - **solution** Lösung - **bulb** "Glühbirne," -lampe - **rated at** hier: mit einer Nennspannung von - **slim** gering, dürftig; auch: schlank - **rating** Bemessung, Auslegung - **average** Durchschnitt - **electricity board** Elektrizitätsbehörde - **mean** hier: Mittelwert - **sub** hier: Verteil..., Unter... - **adequate** ausreichend, genügend - **to push out** hier: unterdrücken - **to cope with** fertigwerden mit - **fluctuation** Schwankung - **to cause** verursachen, bewirken - **peak demand** Höchstbedarf, Spitzenbedarf - **slack** schwach, gering; sonst auch: schlaff, locker - **period** Zeitraum, Periode

### Fuel-cell engine ready for the industry

Sir William Grove, a famous barrister, invented the fuel cell in 1839, but only now has it made the transition from 19th-century curiosity to the ultimate in clean-car technology.

The Canadian company Ballard Power Systems announced last month that this silent energy source, which emits only water vapour, has achieved the power density—power per weight and volume—required for use in a car.

The claim was made at the International Grove Fuel Cell Conference in London. Ballard, based in Vancouver, developed the cell under a joint programme with Daimler-Benz.

According to Mr. Firoz Rasul, Ballard's chief executive, the US Department of Energy had estimated that a fuel-cell engine should

eventually cost about the same as an internal combustion engine of the same volume. Sir William's invention exploits the energy given off by the chemical reactions of burning, in this case the burning that results from the strong affinity of oxygen for hydrogen. However, in the fuel cell the energy comes out as electricity, not fire, because the electrons that pass from one element to another in the reaction are harnessed by an external circuit. With few moving parts, the fuel cell is quiet and demands little maintenance. The new cell is capable of producing 1,000 watts per litre and 700 watts per kilogram, or over 28 kilowatts per cubic foot.
(Weekly Telegraph, London)

**fuel cell** Brennstoffzelle; Stromquelle, in der durch elektrochemische Oxidation ("kalte Verbrennung") von Brennstoff mit Sauerstoff chemische Energie direkt in elektrische Energie umgewandelt wird - **engine** Motor; sonst auch: Triebwerk - **barrister** Anwalt - **to invent** erfinden - **transition** Übergang, Durchgang - **to announce** ankündigen, verkünden - **energy**

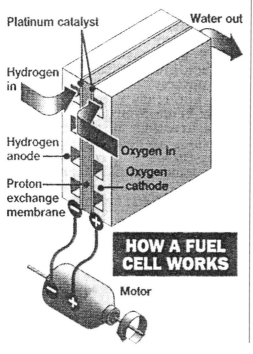

**source** Energiequelle - **to emit** abgeben, emittieren - **water vapo(u)r** Wasserdampf - **to achieve** erreichen, gelangen zu - **power density** Leistungsdichte - **weight** Gewicht - **required** erforderlich, nötig - **claim** Bekanntgabe; auch: Behauptung, Anspruch - **to develop** entwickeln - **joint** gemeinsam - **chief executive** Generaldirektor - **to estimate** schätzen, vermuten - **eventual(ly)** letzten Endes, einaml - **internal combustion engine** Verbrennungskraftmaschine - **to exploit** nutzen, ausbeuten - **to result from** sich ergeben aus, resultieren - **oxygen** Sauerstoff - **hydrogen** Wasserstoff - **to harness** nutzen, verwenden, einspannen - **external circuit** Aussen(strom)kreis - **to demand** verlangen, fordern - **maintenance** Wartung


## Significant reduction of diesel exhausts

Inspired by physics of the upper atmosphere, a group of German researchers has devised a way to cut dramatically the toxic emissions of nitrogen oxides and sulphur dioxide from diesel engines. Their experimental system pumps an electric current through the exhaust gases to render the pollutants harmless.
In Britain, diesel engines present a growing pollution hazard as the number of cars with diesel engines on the road continues to increase. According to the Society of Motor Traders and manufacturers, 22.5 per cent of all new cars last year were powered by diesel engines.
Diesel vehicles produce less carbon monoxide and carbon dioxide than their petrol-burning equivalents, but they generate larger amounts of nitrogen oxides and sulphur dioxide.
The German system for reducing pollutants is being developed by Klaus Pochner and co-workers at the Fraunhofer Institute for Laser Technology in Aachen. Instead of trying to build a catalytic converter, they fitted electrodes into the engine's exhaust system. A current passes between the electrodes, producing a shower of sparks which ionise the exhaust gases to produce nitrogen, oxygen and sulphur.
"You can remove 95 per cent of nitrogen oxides if you use enough energy," says Pochner, "and this system will also work on lean-burn petrol engines."
(Excerpt from New Scientist, London)

significant bedeutsam, wichtig - **exhausts** Abgase - **to devise** ersinnen, sich ausdenken - **to cut** hier: verringern - **toxic** Schadstoff..., giftig - **nitrogen** Stickstoff... - **sulphur** Schwefel... - **current** Strom - **to render** es schaffen, machen - **pollutants** Schadstoffe, Verunreinigungen - **to present** darstellen - **hazard** Gefahr - **to increase** sich erhöhen - **carbon** Kohlenstoff... - **petrol-burning** mit Benzin arbeitend - **to generate** erzeugen - **to develop** entwickeln - **catalytic converter** Katalysator - **to fit** einbauen, montieren, einsetzen, vorsehen - **shower of sparks** Funkenregen - **oxygen** Sauerstoff - **lean-burn petrol engine** Benzin-"Magermotor"

**MTU diesel engines for fast ferry**

The shipbuilders Mjellem & Karlsen of Norway have ordered four 20-cylinder MTU engines for a new 95-metre single-hulled ferry. This will be the first time that MTU has supplied the Series 1163 engines for use in a fast ferry.
The four engines have a combined power of 23,200 kW, or almost 32,000 HP, which will enable the ferry to cut through four-metre high waves at cruising speeds of up to 30 knots. Maximum speed will be 35 knots. Lohmann & Stolterfoht gearboxes will transfer the power to KaMeWa waterjets. The ferry operator, shipping company Driftsselskabet Grenaa-Hundested, is planning to have the ship in service between the Danish islands of Jylland. The three decks will offer space for 600 passengers and 160 cars. Alternatively, the vessel will be capable of taking up to twelve buses or lorries if the number of cars is reduced.
(The Motor Ship, London)

**fast ferry** Schnellfähre, schnelle Fähre - **to order** bestellen - **single-hulled** mit einem Rumpf; hull auch: (Schiffs-)Körper - **to supply** liefern - **to enable** ermöglichen, in den Stand setzen, befähigen - **cruising speed** Reisegeschwindigkeit, Marschfahrt - **knot** Knoten: 1,852 km/h - **gearbox** Getriebekasten - **to transfer** übertragen - **waterjet** Wasserdüse - **ferry operator** Betreiber der Fährlinie - **shipping company** Reederei - **to offer** bieten - **space** Platz, Raum - **lorry** Last(kraft)wagen

**Meteorite showered town with diamonds**

Thousands of tonnes of diamonds discovered beneath a medieval town in Bavaria are forcing experts to rethink their theories how diamonds form.
The walled town of Nördlingen, with 20,000 inhabitants, is built within the Ries crater, one of the best-studied impact craters in the world. Until recently, no one knew that the rocks within the crater contained diamonds. Now a team of British researchers led by Ian Gilmour and Colin Pillinger of the Open University, which discovered the precious stones last year, has analysed the deposits.
Their results suggest that diamond and silicon carbide aggregates form when the plume of vapour or ionised gas created by the meteorite cools and condenses.
The work challenges the best previous theory about how diamonds form. The theory said they are the product of shock-induced transforming of graphite, another form of carbon.
The Ries crater is about twenty-four kilometres across and was gouged out of the rock some 14.7 million years ago by a meteorite. The impact was so great that the fireball blasted through 600 to 700 metres of sedimentary rocks before entering older crystalline rocks in the basement. Gilmour estimates that there are some 72,000 tonnes of diamonds within the Ries crater. Bad news for fortune hunters. The biggest diamonds are only 200 micrometres in diameter.
(Excerpt from New Scientist, London)

**to shower with** überschütten mit - **diamond** Diamant - **to discover** entdecken - **medieval** mittelalterlich - **to rethink** überdenken - **to form** sich bilden, entstehen - **impact crater** Einschlagkrater - **to contain** enthalten - **precious stone** Edelstein; precious auch: wertvoll - **deposit** Ablagerung, Lager - **result** Ergebnis, Resultat - **to suggest** vermuten lassen; sonst auch: vorschlagen - **silicon** Silizium - **carbide** Karbid - **aggregate** Anhäufung, Aggregat - **plume of vapo(u)r** Dampfstreifen; plume auch: Feder, Rauchfahne - **to create** entstehen, schaffen, kreieren - **to challenge** herausfordern - **previous** bestehend, vorherig - **shock-induced** durch Schock verursacht (oder: herbeigeführt) - **across** im Durchmesser - **to gouge** aushöhlen

54

- **impact** Einschlag; auch: Aufprall, Aufschlag - **to blast through** durchblasen, durchfegen - **sedimentary** Sediment(gestein), Ablagerung von Gestein - **basement** (im tiefen) Boden - **to estimate** schätzen - **fortune hunter** Glücksritter; auch: Mitgiftjäger- **diameter** Durchmesser

**Increasing demand for cruise vessels**

Huge 70,000-tonners carrying far more than 2,000 passengers are becoming commonplace. Traditional are they not; some look more like Miami Beach apartment blocks than the ships of yesterday. But they are comfortable, efficient and crammed with high technology.
One of the latest cruising events was the maiden voyage of P&O's 67,000-ton 'Oriana'. A dozen or so new megaships over the 50,000-ton mark will enter service in the next two years, costing a couple of hundred million sterling apiece, and carrying anything from a thousand to two thousand passengers.
Older vessels like Cunard's 'Queen Elizabeth 2' and P&O's 'Canberra' still enjoy megastar status. Many aging Clyde-built veterans are still earning their keep as cruise liners, making up for the lack of youth with their reassuring brass-and-teak charm. Even the gigantic liner 'United States' may return to the cruise circuit after a quarter of a century in mothballs.
There are jazz cruises, bridge-playing cruises and photography cruises. There are also Polar cruises on Russian icebreakers. And there are hairy-chested adventure cruises where dressing for dinner means duffel coats and seaboots.
Somewhere in the middle of all this niche marketing are the great majority of cruises, aimed at the huge middle-class, middle-income market of cruise passengers from a score of nations.
(Excerpt from 'High Life' of British Airways)

**increasing** ansteigend, wachsend - **demand** Nachfrage, Bedarf, Forderung - **cruise vessel** Kreuzfahrtschiff - **commonplace** alltäglich - **efficient** leistungsfähig, effektiv - **crammed** vollgestopft - **cruising event** Ereignis bei der Kreuzfahrerei - **maiden voyage** Jungfernreise - **to enjoy** sich erfreuen - **to earn the keep** sein Geld verdienen - **to make up for** wettmachen, ausgleichen - **lack of youth** das

Fehlen der Neuheit (oder: der Jugend) - **reassuring** beruhigend - **brass-and-teak** Messing und Teakholz - **cruise circuit** Kreuzfahrtroute; circuit sonst auch: Stromkreis, Wasserkreis, Kreislauf - **mothball** Mottenkugel - **hairy-chested** halsbrecherisch, gefährlich, riskant - **aimed at** abzielend auf, absehend auf - **score** Menge, enorme Anzahl

**Market for well-maintained engines**

Fumes from diesel engines may well cause cancer, as the Royal Commission pointed out this autumn. But the concern is not new. "Throughout 1955 and the early part of 1956 there was a recurring suggestion that exhaust gas from diesel engines was an important factor to lung cancer," said London Transport's annual report for 1956.
Local authorities in London were so worried about it that they pressed London Transport to keep its electric trolleybuses and not to replace them with diesel-engined polluters.
However: "Investigations by Research Council's group for research on atmospheric pollution, in which London Transport willingly cooperated, confirmed that the exhaust from a well-maintained diesel engine constitutes no danger to health."
The upshot of this fortuitous research result was that, take a deep breath, London Transport ordered 850 diesel-engined buses to replace the trolleybuses.
(Excerpt from New Scientist, London)

**well-maintained** gut erhalten und gepflegt - **engine** (Diesel-)Motor - **fume** unangenehmer Rauch, Dampf - **to cause** verursachen, bewirken - **to point out** darauf hinweisen, feststellen - **concern** Besorgnis, Sorge - **recurring** wiederkehrend, immer wieder auftretend - **suggestion** Meinung; sonst auch: Vorschlag - **exhaust gas** Abgas - **annual** jährlich, Jahres... - **authority** Verwaltung, Behörde - **to replace** ersetzen - **polluter** (Umwelt-)Verschmutzer, Umweltverseucher - **investigation** Untersuchung - **research council** Forschungsrat, -komitee - **pollution** (Umwelt-)Verschmutzung - **to confirm** bestätigen, bekräftigen - **to constitute** bilden, darstellen - **upshot** Fazit, Endergebnis - **fortuitous** zufällig

55

## American travellers abroad

The American Institute of Electronic and Electrical Engineers, New York, published a newsletter to their members giving advice how to behave abroad.
- Dress in conservative, casual clothes in order to avoid calling attention to yourself.
- Don't wear expensive jewelry, furs, etc., carry expensive cameras or otherwise advertise affluence.
- Don't wear clothing or jewelry advertising your U.S. affiliation or religion. Don't carry religious or political books, magazines or cards.
- Don't tell strangers the name of your company or what business you're in. If attending a work-related meeting, don't wear identification badges in public. If you must bring corporate or government ID on your trip, carry it in your checked baggage.
- Don't disclose your itinerary or hotel plans to strangers, but make sure that someone you trust is advised of your daily travel plans.
- Obtain maps and detailed directions for your destinations. Avoid getting lost. Upon arrival in a city, locate the nearest police station and American consulate or embassy.
- Stay alert and sober at all times.
- Allow plenty of time (at least two hours) for security checks for international flights, both at home and abroad. Be prepared for intense security measures, also answering questions, filling out forms, having your luggage searched and being frisked.
- Don't linger in crowded public access areas. Go directly to your airline's baggage and passenger check-in counter, clear security and wait near the departure gate. People in the boarding areas have already passed through security checkpoints.
- Never make wisecracks in the vicinity of security checkpoints.
(IEEE Newsletter, New York)

**advice** Rat(schlag) - **to behave** sich verhalten - **casual** nicht auffällig, salopp, sportlich - **to avoid** vermeiden - **to wear** tragen - **to advertise affluence** Wohlhabenheit zur Schau stellen - **affiliation** Zugehörigkeit - **to attend** besuchen, beiwohnen, teilhaben - **work-related** die Arbeit betreffend, zur Arbeit gehörend - **identification badge** Abzeichen (oder: Schild) zur Identifikation, Zeichen zur Erkennung - **corporate** betreffend eines Unternehmens - **to disclose** preisgeben, aufdecken - **itinerary** Reiseziel - **to trust** vertrauen - **to advise** unterrichten, mitteilen - **to obtain** sich beschaffen, erhalten - **destination** Zielort - **to get lost** Orientierung verlieren, sich verlaufen - **to locate** hier: den Sitz festellen, lokalisieren - **embassy** Botschaft - **to stay alert** wachsam bleiben, auf der Hut sein - **sober** nüchtern - **measure** Vorkehrung - **to be frisked** durchsucht sein ("gefilzt") - **to linger** verweilen, zurückbleiben - **public access area** Räumlichkeiten für öffentlichen Zugang - **wisecracks** schlaue Bemerkungen, Witzeleien - **vicinity** Nähe, Umfeld

Yes, I do understand. Technical literature from VDI-Verlag excellent.
You may also obtain the catalogue:
VDI-Verlag GmbH, P. B. 10 10 54, D-40001 Düsseldorf

## Low-speed engines for ship's propulsion

All ships being built today are driven by diesel engines. Exceptions are large naval vessels which are propelled by turbines. The latest commercially-operated turbine ship delivered to a shipping company was in 1985.
A survey of "The Motor Ship" on propulsion machinery stated the world's major engine builders:
1. MAN-B&W, 2. Sulzer, 3. Mitsubishi, 4. Pielstick, 5. Wärtsäla, 6. MaK.
However, in the range of large low-speed engines, the following builders dominated the world for ship's propulsion in 1995: MAN-B&W installed 340 ships, Sulzer more than 200, Mitsubishi nearly 100.
(Excerpt from The Motor Ship, London)

**low-speed engine** langsamlaufender Motor - **ship's propulsion** Schiffsantrieb - **built** (to build) gebaut - **exception** Ausnahme - **naval vessel** Schiff der Marine - **commercially-operated** kommerziell betrieben - **to deliver** abliefern - **shipping company** Reederei - **survey** Untersuchung, Überprüfung, Analyse - **propulsion machinery** Antriebsmaschinerie - **to state** feststellen, angeben - **major** Haupt..., wichtig(st) - **engine builder** Hersteller von (Diesel-)Motoren - **range** Reihe, Bereich - **to dominate** beherrschen, dominieren

## Saving millions on EU translations

Each year the European Community spends $190 million to have reams of documents translated into the Community's ten official languages. Despite a 3000-person staff of translators, however, the process is sluggish and translated bills often do not reach members of the European Parliament until just before they must be voted on.
Now a British association of 40 translation companies has suggested that the Common Market could reduce its costs by up to 80 per cent by eliminating its official staff and using private experts. British members are thinking of such a system, in which documents would be transmitted electronically to London, where translators using computers would quickly process the text and send it back.
(Excerpt from Newsweek, New York)

**community** Gemeinschaft - **ream** Bogen von Papier - **staff** Personal; auch: Stab - **process** Vorgang, Prozess - **sluggish** träge, langsam, schwerfällig - **bill** (Gesetzes-)Vorlage, Schrift - **to vote** abstimmen - **association** Gesellschaft - **to suggest** vorschlagen; auch: planen - **to reduce** reduzieren, verringern - **to eliminate** - entlassen, eliminieren - **to transmit** senden - **to process** verarbeiten

## Panama Canal, an engineering marvel

Eighty years after it opened to link the Atlantic and Pacific oceans, the Panama Canal remains one of the engineering marvels in the world. At one end of the 50-mile-long waterway, the 12,000 ships that traverse it annually are lifted 85 ft. above sea level by a series of locks, enabling them to sail through the mountainous spine of the Panama Isthmus. When they reach the opposite coast, another set of locks floats them gently down the ocean.
The operation of these aquatic elevators needs a prodigious amount of fresh water. Each time a ship passes through the canal, some 52 million gallons must be pumped into the locks and then, after the ship has passed, flushed out to sea. "The locks are like giant water closets," explains an official of the Panama Canal commission. "Once you pull the chain, you never see the water again."
For years the source of that water seemed inexhaustible. Much of it comes from dam-created Gatun Lake (165 sq.-mi.), through which the ships pass on their route across the isthmus. Most of the remainder is tapped from nearby Madden Lake, formed in 1935, also by damming, to provide an additional reservoir of water for the dry season.
But now a 375-page report by Stanley Heckadon Moreno, has raised a startling worry about the canal's future: it may be running short of water. Another study shows that silt accumulating at the bottom of the lake has reduced its capacity by 5 per cent. By the year 2000 the loss could be as high as 10 per cent
(Excerpt from TIME, New York)

**engineering marvel** Wunder der Technik - **to link** verbinden - **to traverse** durchfahren, durchqueren - **to lift** (an)heben - **ft.** (foot) 0,3048 m - **lock** Schleuse - **to enable** in den Stand setzen, ermöglichen - **mountainous**

57

gebirgig - **spine** (Gebirgs-)Grat; sonst auch: Rückgrat - **Isthmus** Landenge - **opposite** gegenüberliegend, entgegengesetzt - **to float down** abwärts schwimmen lassen - **aquatic elevator** Wasserfahrstuhl - **prodigious** riesig, gewaltig, ungeheuer - **gallon** GB: 4,5459 l; US: 3,7853 l - **to flush out** hinunterspülen - **giant** riesig, gigantisch - **to pull the chain** die Kette ziehen - **source** Quelle, Ursprung - **inexhaustible** unerschöpflich - **dam-created** durch Dämme geschaffen - **remainder** verbleibendes Wasser - **to tap** (an)zapfen - **to form** bilden - **to provide** vorsehen, liefern - **additional** zusätzlich - **to raise worry** Bedenken (oder: Sorgen) aufkommen lassen - **startling** erschreckend, bestürzend - **silt** Schlamm; sonst auch: Treibsand - **to accumulate** sich ansammeln - **bottom** Grund, Boden

### History lessons

Business Week 1958: "With over 50 foreign cars already on sale here, the Japanese auto industry is not likely to carve out a big slice of the U.S. market."

Frank Knox, U.S. Secretary of the Navy, on December 4, 1941: "Whatever happens, the U.S. Navy is not going to be caught napping."

Marshal Ferdinand Foch in 1911: "Airplanes are interesting toys, but they have no military value."

Economist Irving Fisher on October 16, 1929: "Stocks have reached what looks like a permanent high plateau."

**to carve out** abbekommen, sich abschneiden - **slice** Stück, Scheibe - **secretary of the navy** Marineminister - **napping** unachtsam, nicht auf der Hut, schlafend - **value** Wert - **stock** Aktie, Wertpapier

### Gas for UFO

A service-station attendant watching a Martian put gas into its spacecraft noticed that UFO was printed on the spaceship's side.
"Does that stand for Unidentified Flying Object?" he asked the Martian.

"No," the Martian replied. "Unleaded Fuel Only." (The Chicagoer)

**service-station attendant** Tankwart; in GB: filling-station attendant - **Martian** Bewohner des Mars - **spacecraft** Raumfahrzeug - **to notice** bemerken, feststellen - **unidentified flying object** unbekanntes Flugobjekt - **unleaded fuel** bleifreier Kraftstoff

### Such is business

The development of a new product is a three-step process. First, a U.S. firm announces an invention; second, the Russians claim that they made the same discovery twenty years ago; third, the Japanese start exporting it.

**such is** das nennt sich, so ist nun mal - **development** Entwicklung - **three-step** Dreistufen..., dreistufig - **process** Vorgang, Prozess - **to announce** ankündigen, verkünden - **invention** Erfindung - **to claim** behaupten, beanspruchen - **discovery** Entdeckung

### Being up to date

First Irishman: "Do you have contemporary furniture?" Second Irishman: "Contemporary furniture is out of date."

**contemporary** zeitgenössisch - **furniture** Möbel, Mobilar

### Mind your language

World Francophony Day, in case you did not notice, was on March 20th. President Jacques Chirac refers in most of his foreign-policy speeches to the need, as a "priority," to defend "La Francophony," a nebulous assortment of countries from Congo to Cambodia that enjoy "shared use of the French language." Most Frenchmen seem unaware of this attempt to create a kind of Commonwealth and care even less. Yet it forms a big part of France's ever-growing arsenal of outfits and measures to protect its native tongue against the perceived threat of the global tyranny of English.

Set up ten years ago by President Mitterand with 42 founding member states, Francophonia now has 53 members, four fewer than the Commonwealth, the club of former ex-British territories.

But such is the desperation of the chief mother-tongue-waggering that no qualification is required for entry. French does not have to be country's dominant or official language. In some countries, such as Moldovia, the newest member, hardly any French is spoken at all. For France, which foots the bulk of the Francophonic bill, with plans this year to spend FFr5.6 billion ($1.1 billion) on gambits abroad, the more members the club attracts, the greater its scope for promoting France's language and influence. No fuss about who joins.

As the first language of perhaps 100m people and the occasional language of another 30m-40m, French ranks only ninth in the world, behind not just Chinese, Hindustani, Russian and English, but also Spanish, Arabic, Bengali and Portuguese. But French is still used, at French insistence, as one of the two official languages of all international bodies.

A losing battle. Almost everywhere, English is being adopted as the "lingua franca." At the United Nations only a tenth of the documents is produced in French. All computer programs are in English.

(Excerpt from The Economist, London)

**Francophony Day** Tag der französischen Sprache; oder: Tag der Französischsprachigen - **to notice** bemerken - **to refer to** beziehen sich auf - **priority** Priorität - **to defend** verteidigen - **nebulous** verschwommen, nebelhaft, nebelig - **assortment** Auswahl; auch: Zusammenstellung, Sortierung - **to share** Anteilt haben, teilen - **unaware** unbemerkt - **attempt** Versuch - **to create** schaffen, kreieren - **to form** bilden - **arsenal** Zeughaus, Waffenlager - **outfits** Ausstattung, Ausrüstung - **measures** Massnahmen - **native tongue** Muttersprache, Sprache der Eingeborenen - **to perceive** wahrnehmen, erkennen - **threat** Bedrohung - **tyranny** Despotismus, Tyrannei, Willkürherrschaft - **to set up** einrichten, aufstellen - **founding member states** Staaten der Gründungsmitglieder - **desperation** Verzweifelung - **waggering** Schalkhaftigkeit, Schelmerei - **required** erforderlich, benötigt - **to foot the bulk** die Masse ausmachen, das Gros darstellen - **bill** Vorlage; auch: Gesetz - **gambit** raffinierter Trick; sonst auch: erster Schritt, Eröffnung - **scope** Umfang - **to promote** fördern - **influence** Einfluss - **fuss** unnötige Aufregung, "Wirbel" - **to join** beitreten - **occasional** gelegentlich, Zweit... - **to rank** in der Reihenfolge sein, rangieren - **insistence** Nachdruck, Beharren - **bodies** Körperschafen - **to adopt** zu eigen machen, annehmen, übernehmen

**And please let me have a copy of this message.**

## A stake in the company

Sir—You overlook the victims of downsizing, the white-collar workers, who remain on the job and are expected not only to complete their own work, but also to do all the work that was formerly done by their "outplaced" colleagues. Downsizing is a fad; rational analysis of the corporation seems to follow downsizing, if it occurs at all; and white layoffs, increased workloads and shrinking real wages are hurting the lower ranks, executives are being rewarded with compensation packages beyond any possible justification.

When AT&T announced plans to lay off 40,000 workers, it admitted it had no idea where the cuts would come from. Clearly, someone picked a number that he thought would please Wall Street (it did) and make AT&T a player in the current fad. Companies are destroying employee loyalty, customer relations and whole communities, simply to show they are on their toes by following the latest gimmick of corporate consultants.

Because of this haphazard approach, employees are being dumped without any reduction in the work the organisation is expected to handle. The result is employees whose morale is destroyed by an excessive workload, insecurity and fear. The great gains in technology have added work, not reduced it. and made the work more rigid, confining and unrewarding.

Donald McKinsey, Columbia, South Carolina
(Letters to the Editor, Newsweek, New York)

**stake** Einsatz, Anteil; auch: Gewinn - **victim** Opfer - **downsizing** Verkleinerung einer Firma (durch Entlassung von Mitarbeitern) - **white-collar workers** Angestellte - **to remain** bleiben - **to complete** ausführen, fertigstellen, beenden - **former(ly)** vorher, früher - **outplaced** entlassen - **fad** Marotte; sonst auch: Modetorheit - **to occur** auftreten, vorkommen - **layoff** zeitweise Entlassung - **increased** erhöht - **workload** Arbeitslast - **shrinking** schrumpfend - **real wages** reale Löhne, Realeinkommen - **to hurt** schmerzen - **lower ranks** untere Einkommensklassen - **executive** etwa: Chef, Direktor - **to reward** belohnen - **package** hier: Pauschalbetrag - **justification** Rechtfertigung - **to announce** ankündigen, verkünden, bekanntgeben - **to admit** zugeben, zugestehen - **to pick** (heraus)picken - **current** momentan - **to destroy** zerstören - **employee loyalty** Firmentreue - **customer relations** Kundenbeziehungen - **community** "Knüller" - **corporate consultant** Konsulent, Firmenberater - **haphazard** willkürlich, planlos - **approach** Vorgehensweise, Methode - **to dump** abschieben, loswerden - **to handle** handhaben, bewältigen - **gain(s)** Gewinn - **rigid** starr, unbeweglich - **confining** hier etwa: schmalspurig, einengend, begrenzt - **unrewarding** hier: nicht genügend anerkannt, unbefriedigend

## Copping it from lead

The American gun firm Smith and Wesson is making bullets wrapped in nylon. This is not to keep them warm, but to cut down on a novel form of lead poisoning. Research has shown that policemen suffer from headaches and dizziness after prolonged firing practice; this is because of the lead their weapons release into the atmosphere.

This innovation ensures lead particles cannot escape after the bullet has lodged in its target. New York's Mount Sinai School of Medicine has tested the new bullets, and found they cut lead emissions from pistols by 70% to 80%. The school previously came up with some alarming results which indicated that, if the British TV image of policemen in the U.S. is true, then lead poisoning could be at least to blame. More than half of 81 policemen tested in New York had high levels of lead in the blood after target practice.

The atmospheric lead causes headaches, dizzy spells, insomnia and irritability. Loss of weight and stomach problems were also reported by a fifth of the policemen tested. And out of the 16 fire-arms instructors examined, five had "clear biochemical lead-induced abnormalities," says the school.
(New Scientist, London)

**to cop it** etwas abbekommen, erwischen - **gun firm** Waffenhersteller - **bullet** (sprich: bulit) (Gewehr-)Kugel, Geschoss - **to wrap** hüllen, einwickeln, einpacken - **to cut down on** verringern von - **novel** (neu)artig - **lead poisoning** Bleivergiftung - **to suffer from** leiden an (oder: unter) - **headaches** Kopfweh -

**dizziness** Schwindelgefühl, Benommenheit - **prolonged** langzeitig - **firing practice** Schiessübung - **weapon** Waffe - **to release** abgeben, freigeben - **innovation** Neuheit, Erneuerung - **to ensure** gewährleisten, sichern - **to escape** entkommen - **to lodge** treffen; auch: landen - **target** Ziel - **previous(ly)** früher, vorher - **alarming** beunruhigend, alarmierend - **result** Ergebnis, Resultat - **to indicate** aufzeigen, anzeigen - **image** Bild, Vorstellung - **to blame** Schuld geben; auch: tadeln, rühmen - **level** Niveau - **to cause** verursachen, bewirken - **dizzy spells** Schwindelanfälle - **insomnia** Schlaflosigkeit - **irritability** Gereiztheit - **loss of weight** Gewichtsverlust - **stomach** Magen... - **firearms instructor** Schiessausbilder - **lead-induced** auf Blei zurückzuführen

**America cracks down on illegal spy gear**

You're in a tense negotiation, and the other side just won't budge on the price. What's a fast-thinking business person to do? One idea, made possible by Japan's Micro Electronics Industrial Co, Ltd., is to invent some reason for a short absence, then leave your PK-300 ballpoint pen on the conference table. They'll never guess it's a miniature transmitter.
Out of the room, you can pull out your KZ-100 "reliable pocket partner" receiver, and tune in to the other side's conversation.
Alternatively, you present your negotiating partner with a handy CAL-205 desk calculator, also made by Micro. As a calculator, it does the job. But it also contains a microphone and transmits as far as 200 meters. You could, of course, eavesdrop the old-fashioned way, by installing a telephone wiretap, or bugging the conference room. Micro sells that equipment, too. So did many spy shops around the United States, at least until last week. The problem is that these gadgets may violate American law. (Newsweek, New York)

**to crack down on** (also: to clamp down on) scharf durchgreifen bei, hart vorgehen gegen, Razzia durchführen bei - **spy gear** Gerät für Spionagezwecke - **tense** angestrengt, aufgeregt - **negotiation** Verhandlung - **to budge** sich nicht vom Fleck bewegen, nicht abrücken wollen - **to invent** erfinden - **ball-point pen** (GB also: biro) Kugelschreiber - **to guess** es erraten - **transmitter** Sender - **to pull out** herausziehen, auspacken - **reliable** zuverlässig; auch: betriebssicher - **receiver** Empfänger - **to tune in to** (Gerät) einstellen auf; auch: abstimmen - **to present** als Geschenk übergeben - **negotiating partner** Partner in der Verhandlung - **handy** handlich, praktisch - **to contain** enthalten, Raum haben für - **to transmit** senden - **to eavesdrop** belauschen, abhören, horchen - **wiretap** Anzapfstelle für Telefonleitung(en) - **to bug** 'Wanzen' einsetzen - **equipment** Gerät(e), Ausrüstung, Anlage(n) - **spy shop** Geschäft für Spionagegerät - **gadget** Gerät, Apparatur; auch: Kinkerlitzchen - **to violate the law** Gesetze verletzen, dem Gesetz zuwiderhandeln

**DME fuel for future diesel engines**

At present, dimethyl ether (DME) is used as a propellant in aerosol sprays, a replacement for ozone-eating chlorofluorocarbons. Previously it was best known as a chemical step on the road to the production of synthetic fuels, an area the

How to tackle the big problems.

61

Danish Topsoe Company was keen on. Low petrol prices in the 1980s made synthetic fuels unattractive, but this company kept up an interest in the stuff.
In 1991, an inspired Topsoe laboratory assistant named Svend-Erik Mikkelsen decided to take some DME home and try it in his lawnmower. After cutting the grass, he tried the fuel out in a diesel fork-lift at the factory. This experiment worked so well that the engine refused to stop, even when the ignition was switched off and the starter cables removed. Impressed, Mr Mikkelsen's managers let him pursue his tests with researchers at the nearby Technical University of Denmark.
A year later, armed with hard data, Topsoe approached Amoco, an American oil company. This led to a collaboration between Topsoe Amoco and a diesel-engine research institute in Austria called AVL. This convinced the diesel engineers that DME is more than just a flash in the cylinder. Exhausts contain no sulphur, almost no soot and only 20% of the nitrogen oxides that diesel engines produce.
(The Economist, London)

**DME** Dimethyläther - **propellant** Treibmittel, Treibstoff - **replacement** Ersatz(stoff) - **previous(ly)** vorausgehend, früher - **petrol** Benzin... - **inspired** inspiriert, einfallsreich - **to decide** sich entscheiden - **lawnmower** Rasenmäher - **fork-lift** Gabelstapler - **to refuse** nicht aufhören wollen, sich weigern - **ignition** Zündung - **removed** abgeklemmt, entfernt - **to pursue** nachgehen, verfolgen, weiterführen - **to approach** sich wenden an; sonst auch: sich nähern - **led** (to lead) führte - **to convince** überzeugen, überreden - **flash** Strahl, Blitz - **sulphur** Schwefel - **soot** Russ - **nitrogen oxides** Stickstoffoxyd - **to produce** erzeugen, produzieren

**World's largest factory building**

Seen from the gallery where most tourists are herded, a Jumbo Jet on the production line at Boeing's Everett plant in Washington state is an oddly disappointing sight: it looks big, but not overwhelming. This "trompe l'oeil" is achieved only because its surroundings, a wonder in their own, are even bigger.

The 747 factory is the largest building in the world as to volume, encompassing 13.4 m cubic metres (427 m cubic feet) of space. It would be enough to accommodate about 550 Westminster Abbeys. However, unlike its offspring, this factory cannot fly. The enormous objects it produces can, and have therefore shrunk the world. Boeing 747s have carried 1.4 billion passengers, the equivalent of a quarter of the world's population. They have flown more than 29 billion kilometres (18 billion miles).
(Excerpt from The Economist, London)

**gallery** Galerie; auch: Besichtigungsgang - **to herd** zusammenkommen, sich versammeln - **plant** Anlage, Fabrik - **disappointing** enttäuschend - **overwhelming** umwerfend, überwältigend - **trompe l'oeil** (frz.) trügerischer Schein - **to achieve** erreichen - **surroundings** Umgebung, Umfeld - **to encompass** umfassen - **to accommodate** unterbringen, beherbergen - **offspring** Nachkomme - **shrunk** (to shrink) liess schrumpfen -

**The Engineer's common language**

Faced with the rising tide of technical journals in other languages, engineers will have a certain sympathy with Sir Leonard Atkinson who in his presidential address to the Institution of British Engineers thought that they should include a modern language as a compulsory subject in its examinations.
He said: "In this age it has become increasingly important that engineers of all nationalities should be able to communicate clearly."
It is true that most senior foreign engineers seem to be able to speak English but this can sometimes be puzzling to British experts.
A past-president of FEANI (the European Federation of National Bodies of Engineers) once said in an after-dinner speech: Gentlemen, having briefly addressed you in French, I will continue in the engineer's common language, broken English."
(Electrical Review, London)

**to face** sich gegenübersehen, konfrontiert sein - **rising** anschwellend, steigend - **tide** Flut - **technical journal** Fachzeitschrift - **address** hier: Ansprache - **compulsory subject**

Pflichtfach - **increasing(ly)** immer mehr, wachsend - **to communicate** verständigen - **senior** Chef..., älterer - **puzzling** verwirrend - **broken English** gebrochenes Englisch

**Electronic eyes unblinking**

In the name of crime prevention, closed-circuit television cameras are increasingly monitoring anyone who walks on city streets, cashes checks, rides buses or trains, parks a car or attends a sports event. Panning, tilting and swiveling, some cameras can see in the dark and read newspapers at 100m. Police dogs are even fitted with tiny chest cameras to track down dangerous suspects inside buildings.
Fully three-quarters of Britain's authorities are equipped with closed-circuit systems watching over 250 town centers. The use of CCTV is growing part of police efforts to combat crime, soccer hooliganism and terrorism.
But the prying eyes are not always limited to public spaces, and in recent weeks questions of privacy are at last being raised in a country that has generally taken a relaxed view of video monitoring.
"Nowhere in the world is more surveillance or more acceptance of it," says Deputy Chief Constable Richard Thomas of Gwent, in Wales. "European Continentals are much tighter on privacy than we are, and Americans have told me that this sort of coverage would never be accepted in the U.S."
(Excerpt from Newsweek, New York)

**unblinking** ungerührt; auch: unerschrocken - **crime prevention** Verbrechensverhütung - **closed-circuit television** Überwachungs-Fernsehen; closed-circuit auch: geschlossener Kreis(lauf) - **to monitor** überwachen - **to cash checks** Schecks einlösen - **sports event** Sportereignis - **to pan** (Kamera) schwenken - **to tilt** sich neigen - **to swivel** schwenken - **to fit** versehen, ausstatten - **to track down** aufspüren - **suspect** verdächtige Person - **authority** Behörde, Verwaltung - **to equip** ausrüsten - **effort** Bemühen, Anstrengung - **to combat** bekämpfen - **soccer hooliganism** Fussballrauditum - **prying** neugierig, naseweis - **to raise** erheben, aufkommen, beleben - **surveillance** Überwachung - **acceptance** Akzeptanz, Annahme - **deputy** Stellvertreter - **coverage** Überwachung; auch: Abdeckung

**Sweltering in the exhibition halls**

Berlin has been holding its famous International Broadcasting Exhibition since 1924. The show is now subtitled the "World of Consumer Electronics." This year's event drew around half a million visitors willing to pay nearly £10 each to swelter in the thirty or so exhibition halls, and pack like sardines in the garden area where live TV shows are the big draw.
By tradition, German TV companies provide gimmicks to keep the visitors happy in the garden between the events. This year we had real snow imported by satellite channel Eurosport, bungee jumping from a skyscraper crane and a simulated rock face for "abseiling."

There's nothing like computerised office work.

63

But the attraction that caught "Feedback's" eye was something completely different, a Batman flying machine.
An enormous fan, like a jet engine, is buried under a pile of inflatable cushions inside an open-topped mesh cylinder, around ten metres wide and high. A volunteer dons a Caped Crusader suit while an operator turns up the fan to a deafening roar. The volunteer then dives into the stream of air and is lifted as high as a house by the updraft. With practice and careful use of arms and cape, it is possible to hover in flapping suspension for as long as the fan is at full blast.
It struck us that school teachers could use the machine to explain the theories of gravity, dynamics and aero-dynamics all at the same time, and with full classes guaranteed.
("Feedback" in New Scientist, London)

**to swelter** vor Hitze (fast) umkommen, schmachten, in Schweiss baden - **exhibition hall** Ausstellungshalle - **broadcasting exhibition** Funkausstellung - **to subtitle** mit Untertitel versehen - **event** Veranstaltung, Ereignis; auch: Vorfall - **drew** (to draw) zog an - **big draw** grosse Attraktion, Anziehung - **gimmick** Reklamenüller, Aufhänger - **bungee jumping** Mutspringen - **rock face** Felswand - **fan** Ventilator, Gebläse - **jet engine** Düsentriebwerk - **buried** versteckt, untergebracht; sonst auch: begraben - **pile** Stapel, Schicht - **inflatable** aufblasbar - **cushion** Kissen, Matte - **open-topped** oben offen - **mesh cylinder** Maschenzylinder - **volunteer** Freiwilliger, Kandidat - **to don** anziehen, Hut aufsetzen - **caped crusader suit** - Raumfahreranzug - **deafening** Höllen..., ohrenbetäubend - **roar** Getöse - **to hover** schweben - **flapping** hier: mit ausgebreiteten Armen - **suspension** Schwebezustand

**Race for pollution-free engines**

In the race to produce pollution-free vehicles, electric motors powered by fuel cells will one day replace internal combustion engines.
Fuel cells generate electricity by combining hydrogen with oxygen from the air; their only waste product is water.
But the first cars driven by fuel cells may not be all that green, as they are likely to use diesel as a source of their hydrogen, a conference in London heard a few months ago.
The big three American car makers are General Motors, Ford and Chrysler; they all have fuel cell programmes.
Fuel cell designers have a lot more work ahead to increase performance and reduce cost. But car designers want to know now which fuel they will be using. In the long term, everyone agrees, hydrogen will be the fuel of choice.
Liquid hydrogen made from natural gas contains only about half the energy of the gas that springs from the ground. However, this is unacceptable if the aim is to reduce global warming and improve the efficiency with which we use natural resources.
This leaves diesel, which can be oxidised in the car partially to produce hydrogen with negligible emissions of nitrogen oxides. To reduce sulphur dioxide emissions, sulphur would have to be removed at the refinery. But the real advantage is that filling stations already handle diesel.
The Canadian company Ballard already makes buses driven by fuel cells that run on hydrogen. The company's vice-president, Keith Prater, agrees that diesel may be the way forward. "We think it's a very good idea," he said at the conference."
(Excerpt from The Economist, London)

**pollution-free** umweltfreundlich - **powered by** betrieben mittels, angetrieben durch - **fuel cell** Brennstoffzelle - **to replace** ersetzen - **internal combustion engine** Verbrennungs-Kraftmaschine - **to generate** erzeugen - **hydrogen** Wasserstoff - **oxygen** Sauerstoff - **waste product** Abfallprodukt - **source** Quelle, Ursprung - **designer** Konstrukteur - **to increase** erhöhen - **performance** Leistung - **in the long term** auf lange Sicht - **unacceptable** nicht akzeptabel - **efficiency** Leistung; auch: Wirkungsgrad - **negligible** vernachlässigbar - **sulphur** Schwefel - **advantage** Vorteil - **filling station** Tankstelle

**Put an end to toxic fuel**

Environmentalists demand it for years. Now the automotive industry demands it: Benzole must be removed from gasoline and sulphur be taken out of diesel oil.

Benzole is to be reckoned among the worst carcinogenic substances. Every year more than 50000 tons of this colorless, light-volatile matter are being released into the air by motor traffic; this corresponds to the amount laden to a medium-sized tanker. The toxic substance flows out of the filling-tap and escapes unburnt at the exhaust pipe. It may also emerge from chemical reactions when burning the fuel. Measurements in overcrowded areas indicated that the perilous benzole load has been risen dramatically during the last years.
(U.S. News & World Report, New York)

**to put an end to** aufhören mit - **toxic** giftig, Gift... - **fuel** Brennstoff - **environmentalist** Umweltschützer - **to demand** verlangen, fordern - **automotive industry** (US) Automobilindustrie - **to remove** entfernen - **sulphur** Schwefel - **to reckon** zählen, rechnen - **carcinogenic** krebsauslösend - **light-volatile** leichtverflüchtigend - **to release** freigeben - **to correspond** entsprechen - **filling-tap** Zapfhahn - **to escape** entkommen - **exhaust pipe** Auspuffrohr - **to emerge** auftreten, vorkommen - **to indicate** aufzeigen, anzeigen - **perilous** gefährlich - **load** Last, Belastung

**When to transmit Mayday, when SOS?**

Wenn jemand Hilfe in Seenot anfordert, so wird er im Sprechfunk "Mayday" rufen. Dieses Wort

**Just order your own catalogue from VDI-Verlag in Düsseldorf.**

ist abgeleitet aus dem Französischen von "Veuillez m'aider" (Helft mir). Mit einem Maientag hat es gar nichts zu tun.
Mit einem Funk-Morsegerät wird der Mensch in Not SOS senden. Samuel Morse (1791-1872), ein Amerikaner, meldete den Morsetelegrafen 1837 als Patent an. Morse war übrigens einer der berühmtesten amerikanischen Porträtmaler.
(Engineering Report, Nussbaumen)

**Strange place**

In 1989 World Gliding Championships were held at South Cerney in Gloucestershire. Though English is the accepted language in aviation, communication problems often arose with our foreign visitors.
During a cross-country flight, I overheard one of the teams on the radio, advising Base Control in accented English that they had landed in a field but could not pin-point their position for recovery: "We think we located Bourton-on-the-Water, Stow-on-the-Wold and Moreton-in-Marsh."
"Are there any road signs near your landing point?" asked Base. "Yes," came the reply. "We are one mile south of somewhere called Mud-on-the-Road, but we can't find it on our map."
(Alistair Smith in Midland Gazette, England)

**gliding championships** Meisterschaft im Segelfliegen - **aviation** Luftfahrt - **overheard** hörte mit - **to advise** hier: mitteilen - **accented** mit (starkem) Akzent - **to pin-point** genau bestimmen - **for recovery** hier: zum Abholen - **road sign** Hinweisschild, -zeichen - **Mud-on-the-Road** verschmutzte Strasse

**Producing the licence**

The defence counsel for a drunk driver was asking the right questions. The arresting officer had testified that the defendant, when asked to produce his licence, had fumbled around endlessly in the glove compartment.
"But wasn't it dark, and the compartment cluttered?" asked the lawyer. "Yes."
"How long did he fumble around there?"
"Maybe five minutes," responded the officer.
"Well," continued the lawyer, "do you find it unusual that a man would take his time looking

65

in a dark and cluttered glove compartment for a small piece of paper?"
"Yes," replied the officer. "He was in my patrol car at the time."
(James Wellington, Reading News, England)

**to produce** hervorholen; sonst auch: erzeugen - **licence** Fahrausweis, Führerschein - **defence councel** Verteidigung - **drunk** betrunken - **arresting officer** Polizist, der die Festnahme vorgenommen hat - **to testify** bestätigen - **defendant** Angeklagte(r) - **to fumble around** herumfummeln - **glove department** Handschuhfach - **cluttered** nicht aufgeräumt, voller Unordnung - **lawyer** Rechtsanwalt - **patrol car** Streifenwagen

How strong is your car battery?

A neat electronic gadget for checking batteries is now being given away free in Japan with Panasonic batteries.
It is based on a strip of transparent polyester film, with a metallic contact pad at each end. The pads are connected by a strip of resistive material. The strip narrows along its length, so that its electrical resistance varies, patches of liquid-crystal material are printed over the strip.
When you bend the strip over a battery, and hold the two metal contacts against the battery's positive and negative terminals, current flows through the resistive track. This generates heat, with the strip getting hottest where it narrows. The heat makes the liquid-crystal cells glow red or blue.
A fresh, strong battery heats a long section of the strip, and changes the colour of several liquid-crystal cells. A weak battery heats only a short strip and lights only a few cells. A flat battery lights none.
(New Scientist, London)

**gadget** Gerät, Apparatur; auch: Kinkerlitzchen - **strip** Streifen - **contact pad** Kontaktstelle - **to connect** verbinden - **resistive material** Widerstandsmaterial - **to narrow** schmaler (oder: enger) werden - **to vary** sich verändern - **patch** Stück, Abschnitt - **liquid-crystal** Flüssigkristall... - **to bend** biegen - **terminal** Klemme - **current** Strom - **to flow** fliessen - **track** Streifen, Spur - **to generate** erzeugen - **heat** Wärme - **to glow** glühen - **flat** hier: leer

Just for fun

An Irishman went to the cinema. Halfway through the big film another Irishman fell from the balcony to the stalls, landing a few seats from him.
"That was good," he said to himself, "I'll stay and see that part round again."
First Irishman: "What happened to you?"
Irishman on crutches: "I fell out of my wheelchair."

**stalls** Sperrsitz - **to see round again** alles von vorne noch einmal sehen - **crutches** Krücken - **wheelchair** Rollstuhl

Maintenance-free automotive battery
1 One-piece cover
2 Terminal-post cover
3 Cell connector
4 Terminal post
5 Frit
6 Plate strap
7 Case
8 Bottom mounting rail
9 Positive plates, inserted into envelope separators
10 Negative plates

Go ahead, ask for something.

## Methane gas will fuel power stations

The first power station in Britain to run on gas produced by a rubbish tip will join the national grid in about a year's time. The Meriden tip, near Birmingham airport, should produce more than 3.5 megawatts of power, enough for a town of 5000 people.
Packington Estate Enterprises, which manages the tip, will spend £1.5 million on the project, to which the department of energy will add £0.5 million.
Last year, a report recently released by the government estimated that there were at least 660 landfill dumps in Britain capable of producing enough gas to generate useful amounts of power.
Packington estimates that landfill gas could produce five per cent of Britain's electricity. Fermentation in tips produces methane and carbon dioxide. The gas is collected by pipes within the tip.
The gas will be burnt in a gas turbine to drive the station's generators. Gas will first pass through a water scrubber to remove dirt and corrosive gases such as hydrogen sulphide. The scrubber delivers a fuel that has about half the calorific value of natural gas.
A compressor then mixes air with the gas and raises the mixture's pressure to about 20 times that of the atmosphere, at which the gas turbine takes in enough fuel to run efficiently.
(Excerpt from New Scientist, London)

**to fuel** versorgen (mit Brennstoff) - **rubbish tip** Abfall-, Müllhalde - **grid** Verbundnetz - **department of energy** Ministerium für Energie - **to release** veröffentlichen, freigeben - **to estimate** schätzen - **landfill dump** Müllhalde - **capable** imstande; sonst auch: fähig - **fermentation** Gärung - **carbon dioxide** Kohlendioxyd - **water scrubber** Wasserreiniger - **hydrogen sulphide** Wasserstoffsulfid - **value** Wert - **to raise** erhöhen, ansteigen lassen - **to run efficiently** wirtschaftlich arbeiten

## How to handle specifications

It is normal practice to receive specifications which are overspecified. Each customer wants to ensure as much safety in his equipment as possible.
Careful reading and interpreting of customer specifications is one of the most profitable tasks an engineer can perform. For example, both material and labour costs may be reduced by applying the appropriate cable and wire sizes. When control cables in industrial applications are specified 14 AWG (American Wire Gage), the project engineer should convince the customer, utilising the required data from the cable manufacturer, that 1.5 square millimetres is sufficient to perform the task.
14 AWG converted into square millimetres equals 2.08 square millimetres, the next higher diameter size in the cable chart is 2.5 square millimetres, the lower 1.5 square millimetres. This does not mean any devaluation of the system, but savings in large installations in the order of possibly £1 million.
Overspecifying can even degrade the safety of the system. In ship's cable systems, for example, the overrating of cable and other electric equipment adds additional and unwanted weight to the plant. Examples can be found throughout the industry. The larger the plant the more possibilities for savings can be found.
(Engineering Report, Nussbaumen)

**overspecified** überspezifiziert, bei vielen Daten zu hoch ausgelegt - **to ensure** sich versichern, sichern - **profitable** lohnenswert, profitabel - **task** Aufgabe - **to perform** leisten, ausführen - **to apply** verwenden - **appropriate** entsprechend, geeignet, passend - **cable size** Kabelgrösse - **control cable** Steuerkabel - **American Wire Gage** Amerikanische Kabeltabelle - **to convince** überzeugen - **to utilise** verwenden, ausnutzen - **required** erforderlich - **sufficient** genug, ausreichend - **to perform a task** eine Aufgabe erfüllen - **to convert** umwandeln - **diameter size** Querschnittsabmessung - **devaluation** Abwertung - **to degrade** verringern, herabsetzen - **overrating** zu hohes Auslegen

## How to avoid misunderstandings when handling specifications

Even in accurately written specifications and rules misunderstandings can emerge. One of the

# MinProg creativity

## The Ministry of Progress presents a novel self-assessment scheme

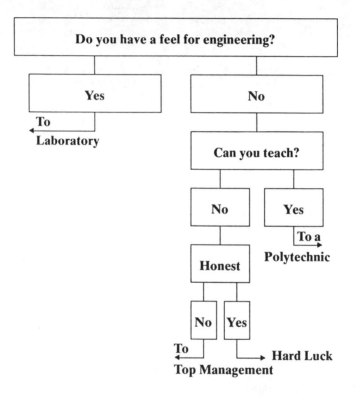

A unique self-assessment scheme has been devised by the Ministry of Progress, Pulham Down. Now you yourself may discover whether you are the right man for the engineering profession.
(Derived from New Scientist, London)

**unique** einzig(artig) — **self-assessment scheme** System der Selbsteinschätzung — **to devise** ersinnen, sich ausdenken — **Ministry of Progress** Ministerium für Fortschritt — **to discover** entdecken

means of preventing misunderstandings is to include key drawings which provide a basic for discussion upon a certain object.
Building and layout plans can be regarded as key plans, as can also one-line diagrams for electrical systems.
It is it easier to speak on the telephone with your counterpart about the equipment if both of you have the same plans with comprehensive data and additional notes before you, not only written words.
Sometimes people call up who have difficulty expressing themselves in English. Those plans which contain much detail will certainly help to overcome possible communication problems. Any customer will be impressed if he receives the data he wants without delay. Furthermore, a detailed question can be answered without having too much paper on the table. It is of great advantage to use scaled-down plans. However, great care must be taken that lettering of suitable size is used. The information on the reduced diagram or sketch might otherwise become illegible.
(Engineering Report, Nussbaumen)

**to avoid** vermeiden - **to handle** handhaben, umgehen mit - **specification** Bauvorschrift, (meist) Spezifikation - **to emerge** vorkommen, auftreten, erscheinen - **to prevent** vermeiden, verhindern - **key drawing** Schlüsselzeichnung - **to provide** vorsehen, darstellen, liefern - **layout plan** Bauplan - **one-line diagram** Übersichtsplan - **counterpart** Gegenüber - **equipment** Gerät(e), Ausrüstung, Anlage(n) - **comprehensive** umfassend - **to overcome** fertigwerden mit - **scaled-down plan** verkleinerter Plan - **lettering** Schriftgrösse - **illegible** unleserlich

## Stopping the eavesdroppers

Eavesdropping on the electromagnetic waves emitted from electrical equipment is a growing problem for banks, insurance companies and other organisations that want to keep their computer data confidential.
These companies know how easy it still is for an eavesdropper to use cheap and relatively simple equipment to pick up spurious fields emanating from computer VDUs. With nothing more than a TV set, aerial and cheap processor, eavesdroppers can capture electromagnetic signals from other people's computers, and see what appears on their VDUs.
The military have known of the problem for over 20 years, and their solution is to build a Faraday cage around electrical equipment holding sensitive information. A Faraday cage is an earthed electrical conductor totally surrounding the equipment. This prevents electromagnetic waves entering and leaving the cage.
The problem for banks and other companies is the cost of constructing a Faraday cage around existing buildings. Another problem present the windows. People operating computers inside Faraday cages have up to now had to work in windowless rooms because these waves can pass easily through glass.
Pilkington Brothers, a British firm of glass manufacturers, has developed a type of glass that, the company says, reduces the amount of electromagnetic radiation that can pass through. The glass is laminated with a very thin layer of indium tin oxide, an electrical conductor. A fine wire mesh around the edges of the pane of glass connects this metallic layer to earth.
(Excerpt from New Scientist, London)

Your driving licence has run out.

**eavesdropper** Lauscher, Horcher - **to emit** abgeben, abstrahlen - **equipment** Gerät, Ausrüstung, Anlage(n) - **confidential** geheim, vertraulich - **spurious** umgebend, abstrahlend - **to emanate** ausstrahlen; auch: ausströmen - **aerial** Antenne - **to capture** einfangen - **to appear** erscheinen - **solution** Lösung - **Faraday cage** Faradayscher Käfig - **sensitive** hier: gefährdet - **earthed** geerdet - **conductor** Leiter - **to surround** umgeben - **to prevent** verhindern - **to contruct** bauen - **to develop** entwickeln - **radiation** Strahlung - **laminated** laminiert, beschichtet - **fine wire mesh** Feinmaschendraht - **edge** Kante - **pane** Scheibe

### Executive of an engineering company

A large engineering company was looking for a replacement of one of their top officials, who was due to retire. Among the candidates who were short-listed was one who seemd to fit the company's requirements in every way. The chairman was delighted. "We'll interview him just for the sake of form," he said, "but I don't think we need look further."
"There's just one thing, though," said one of the members of the committee. "I don't know Mr. Attlee personally. But I have heard that he is inclined to lift his elbow a deal too much. We should make a point of finding out whether this is true."
The day came for the interview. Mr. Attlee was ushered before the committee. The chairman asked a few questions concerning personal details and work experience. The he said, "Now, Mr. Attlee, we would like to ask you a few questions of a different nature. The first thing is: what does the word 'Haig' suggest to you?"

Unhesitatingly, Mr. Attlee replied, "I recall the famous Commander-in-Chief Earl Haig, who led the British forces to victory in France in the First World War."
"Thank you," said the chairman. "And the words White Horse?"
"The Vale of White Horse in Oxfordshire, very beautiful, many happy days I have spent there."
"Splendid," said the chairman. "Just one last question. "What are your reactions to the words VAT 69?"
Mr. Attlee looked a bit baffled. "Ah, there you have me, I'm afraid. Could it be the Pope's telephone number?"
(Electronics & Power, Stevenage, England)

**executive** Chef (in Konzern), Direktor - **replacement** Ersatz, Ersetzung - **top official** Chef in hoher Position - **to retire** in den Ruhestand treten, sich zurückziehen - **short-listed** auf kurzer Liste - **to fit** gerechtwerden, passen - **requirements** Anforderungen - **inclined** geneigt - **to lift the elbow a deal too much** oft einen zuviel heben - **to usher** vorladen, hereinführen - **to suggest** bedeuten, meinen; sonst auch: vorschlagen - **baffled** verwirrt, perplex

### Two Concorde Pilots

It doesn't do to dwell too much on the past, but 19 years ago Concorde, the result of an Anglo-French collaboration in cost-ineffectiveness, started flying fare-paying passengers at twice the speed of sound.
For the first scheduled flight, both the French and British planes took off at exactly the same time, one from London to Bahrain, the other from Paris to Rio. It wasn't put about much at the time, but the French plane soon flew into difficulties.
Two pilots were needed for the flight, and immediately the problem arose of who would sit on the left and be captain.
One of the two pilots chosen had seniority rank, but the other had more flying hours with Concorde. Rank won the day, and the seat on the left, but the pilots took off in high Gallic dudgeon.
Early in the flight, a technical hitch arose, making it impossible for the aircraft to be flown at supersonic speed. Only the pilot on the

We now clamp down on polluters.

right, with the benefit of more flying hours, knew the solution and he wasn't talking to his colleague on the left.
It took a personal radio-telephonic call from the President to re-establish relations and get the plane up to Mach 2.
("Feedback" in New Scientist, London)

**it doesn't do** es lohnt sich nicht, es bringt nichts - **to dwell too much** zu lange zu verweilen - **result** Ergebnis, Resultat - **cost-ineffectiveness** Unwirtschaftlichkeit in den Kosten(dingen) - **fare-paying** zahlend - **speed of sound** Schallgeschwindigkeit - **scheduled flight** geplanter Flug - **it wasn't put about much** es wurde nicht viel darüber geredet - **arose** (to arise) tauchte auf - **seniority rank** die höhere Position, den höheren Grad - **in high dudgeon** sehr aufgebracht - **hitch** Defekt, Fehler; auch: Haken, Ruck - **supersonic speed** Überschallgeschwindigkeit - **benefit** Vorteil, Nutzen - **solution** Lösung - **to re-establish** wieder herstellen - **relations** Beziehungen

### The fizzling of the "Queen Elizabeth 2"

It was to have been a festive day. The 'new' liner "Queen Elizabeth 2" was embarking on a second maiden voyage after a $130 million overhaul that took her out of service for six months.
But like the weather, the planned welcoming festivities fizzled. Instead of a naval gun salute, a local high-school band welcomed the ship with 'Soul Man'. New York's Mayor was nearly an hour late. Worst of all, some 1,300 passengers complained that the voyage was not what it was touted to be. There were problems of flooding in some cabins, broken-down air conditioners in others, an inadequate telephone system and a health club that never opened. In an effort to make amends, Cunard offered a reimbursement to all passengers, a total sum of about $1 million. "That refund will pay for our drinks bill," groused one disembarking man. Despite the grumblings, however most of the passengers gave the ship high marks. Said one intrepid voyager: "If Cunard had canceled the crossing to iron out the kinks, I suppose we would have all been very disappointed.
(Newsweek, New York)

**fizzling** Malheur, kleine Pleite - **festive** festlich, Fest... - **to embark** Passagiere und Ladung aufnehmen; auch: beginnen mit einem Vorhaben - **overhaul** Überholung - **to fizzle** danebengehen, fehlschlagen - **naval** Marine... - **gun salute** Salutschiessen - **to complain** sich beschweren - **to tout** ausrufen, verkünden - **inadequate** unzureichend - **effort** Bemühen, Anstrengung - **to make amends** etwas gutmachen, kompensieren - **reimbursement** Entschädigung, Vergütung, Gutmachung - **refund** Rückzahlung - **to grouse** nörgeln, murren - **to disembark** von Bord gehen, aussteigen - **grumblings** Schimpferei, Murren - **high marks** gute Noten - **intrepid** kühn, unerschrocken - **to cancel** streichen, absagen - **to iron out** ausbügeln - **kinks** hier etwa: Ungereimtheiten; sonst: Knoten, Verzerrungen

**From Weltwoche, Zürich**

# Phonetic alphabets

## Buchstabiertabelle

|   | GB | USA | D (A) | CH |
|---|---|---|---|---|
| A | Andrew | Abel | Anton | Anna |
| B | Benjamin | Baker | Berta | Bertha |
| C | Charlie | Charlie | Cäsar | Cäsar |
| D | David | Dog | Dora | Daniel |
| E | Edward | Easy | Emil | Emil |
| F | Frederick | Fox | Friedrich | Friedrich |
| G | George | George | Gustav | Gustav |
| H | Harry | How | Heinrich | Heinrich |
| I | Isaac | Item | Ida | Ida |
| J | Jack | Jig | Julius | Jakob |
| K | King | King | Kaufmann (Konrad) | Kaiser |
| L | Lucy | Love | Ludwig | Leopold |
| M | Mary | Mike | Martha | Marie |
| N | Nellie | Nan | Nordpol | Niklaus |
| O | Oliver | Oboe | Otto | Otto |
| P | Peter | Peter | Paula | Peter |
| Q | Queenie | Queen | Quelle | Quelle |
| R | Robert | Roger | Richard | Rosa |
| S | Sugar | Sugar | Samuel (Siegfried) | Sophie |
| T | Tommy | Tare | Theodor | Theodor |
| U | Uncle | Uncle | Ulrich | Ulrich |
| V | Victor | Victor | Viktor | Viktor |
| W | William | William | Wilhelm | Wilhelm |
| X | Xmas | X | Xanthippe (Xaver) | Xaver |
| Y | Yellow | Yoke | Ypsilon | Yverdon |
| Z | Zebra | Zebra | Zacharias (Zürich) | Zürich |
| Ä | | | Ärger | |
| Ö | | | Ökonom (Österreich) | |
| Ü | | | Übermut | |
| Ch | | | Charlotte | |
| Sch | | | Schule | |

**For your personal collection of phrases and vocabulary**

"Now we have solved the fly-ash disposal problem."
(Power, New York)

**For your personal collection of phrases and vocabulary**

|   |   |
|---|---|
|   |   |
|   |   |
|   |   |
|   |   |
|   |   |
|   |   |
|   |   |
|   |   |
|   |   |

# At the Ministry of Progress

Brilliant people at the MinProg Secret Service Division in Pulham Down are proud to show their latest major achievements.

**Ministry of Progress** Ministerium für Fortschritt – **major** Haupt . . ., wichtig – **achievement** Leistung, Errungenschaft

**For your personal collection of phrases and vocabulary**

"I just met the most incredible aluminium sliding salesman . . ."

**For your personal collection of phrases and vocabulary**

Novel food tests are being performed at the Ministry of Progress, Pulham Down.

For your personal collection of phrases and vocabulary

**The office of the past**

**The office of the future**

New Scientist, London

# There has been an alarming increase in the number of things I know nothing about. Therefore:

# Engineering Report

**Internationale Monatsschrift für technisches Englisch
Elektrotechnik und Maschinenbau**

Jahresabonnement
Januar bis Dezember:
SFr. 44,– / DM 50,– / ö. S. 380,–
Verlangen Sie ein kostenloses Probeexemplar

Engineering Report
Georg Möllerke
Kornweg 5
CH-5415 Nussbaumen

Drawing by courtesy of Bill Tidy, New Scientist, London and Bill Tidy Ltd., Kegworth, Leicestershire